THEY WEEP ON MY DOORSTEP

Ruth Barnett, an abortionist, between 1918 and 1968 to demonstrate that it was the law, not so-called back alley practioners, that most endangered women's life in the years before abortion was legal.

By Ruth Barnett As Told to Doug Baker Remastered by Andria and Jessica Lask

ISBN: 9798638062903
Imprint: Independently published

Cover design by: Art Painter
Library of Congress Control Number: 2018675309
Printed in the United States of America

This book is dedicated to the women of the world. Theirs alone is the right of decision.

Andria and Jessica Lask are the creators of the movement Hope For Yourself Co. cultivating self-compassion, self-love and self-freedom for all the women and girls of the world. To support our movement— follow on Instagram @hopeforyourself

This book is dedicated to our sweet grandma Ruthie. Till we meet again.

"Decades ago, women suffered through horrifying back-alley abortions. Or, they used dangerous methods when they had no recourse. So when the Republican Party launched an all-out assault on women's health, pushing bills to limit access to vital services, we had to ask: Why is the GOP trying to send women back... to the back alley?"

LISA EDELSTEIN

CONTENTS

FOREWORD

We were expected, so her lawyer sounded the horn a couple of times and the electrically gates swung open to admit the low-slung sports car. She was standing in the doorway as we alighted, five tiny dogs at her heels. Unlike most little dogs, they weren't yapping dogs. They were those little dogs that tend to resemble people, and, like people, they were all different— a Yorkshire, a Chihuahua, a poodle and two others I could not identify. She stood there on the edge of the snowy lawn and, for a long while she didn't recognize me. She isn't always easy to recognize either, except for the shaky legs. She is a strong woman, but her pins are racked by cancer now and she hobbles with a cane. It's the business on the wigs that make her hard to recognize on occasion. That night she was wearing a red-haired wig, but sometimes it is blond and sometimes platinum gray. They say she has 20 of them, maybe even more. Once she was able to focus on us, she welcomed us with the warmth she has always felt for most kinds of people. With her accustomed sympathy for other people's problems, she asked me about my recent boating accident. "I was planning to send you some mallard ducks," she said. "I'll have my housekeeper bake some with wild rice on Friday and I'll send them over." I must have had a strange look on my face, because she sensed immediately that something was wrong. I turned to her lawyer and I said, "I'm afraid your lawyer has other plans for you." Her attorney, a patient, scholarly man, tried to be gentle, but being a realist, he

was preparing her for the worst. It was rather grim to sit there in that black and red kitchen with the.

Oriental motif and hear the slow unfolding of what could be a death sentence. "You have to be in court in the morning, Ruth," he said. "We have run the race and the horse is tired. I have spent hours and hours working on your case. I've talked to the district attorney and I've talked to the judge. I'm in a terrible position and I can't file a written motion. You may have to go to Salem tomorrow." At first she was incredulous. It is hard for a 74-year-old woman beset with the malignancy to grasp the enormity of entering a penitentiary in another 12 or 14 hours. And it had been many years since Ruth Barnett Bush served her last jail sentence at Rocky Butte. Her trial on the charge in question was in June of 1966. Since then there had been a long series of appeals and writs and motions and legal arguments. Even when the Oregon Supreme Court confirmed her sentence of 18 months early in December of 1967, it still had not seemed real to her. After all, she had tried twice since that time by juries and, in one case, has escaped with a fine. "You're too much of a gentleman," she told her lawyer. "You're too ethical. You should get up in court and tell these people what I think of them." "It wouldn't do any good, Ruth," said the lawyers. "All the shouting in the world won't change the laws. It's been nearly two years. The horse is tired and the race is over. She said she wanted her granddaughter to hear it again and called young Ruthie into the kitchen. The lawyer once again explained how each appeal and legal maneuver had been exhausted. There was a long silence in the kitchen, broken only by the fussing of the pack of toy dogs. After a time, her old equilibrium returned. She asked her lawyer if she could get another 10 days to take care of her financial affairs and to enter a hospital for a necessary treatment. He said he would try, but he could promise her nothing.

It was an election year, he explained, and the district attorney would oppose any further stay of sentence. So, she called a friend in law enforcement and asked what she could take with

her to Salem. "Only a pair of flats," she repeated to us. "No cosmetics, not even my girdle." She put down the telephone and asked, "I wonder if I could get away with just one wig if I wore it. I suppose they would find out it was a wig." Because I had never before seen a 74-year-old woman with cancer sent to the Oregon penitentiary (and, because I am rather partial to this oddly dedicated woman), I showed up in Circuit Judge Dean Bryson's court at 9 a.m. the next morning to see the State of Oregon exact its ounce of flesh. Judge Bryson, as always, was meticulously fair. He listened while Ruth's lawyer asked for a moderation of sentence. "What are we going to gain by locking her up?" he asked. A deputy district attorney countered with the assertion that "Mrs. Barnett seems unable to stop her criminal activities." Mrs. Bush's physician took the stand to say that in addition to the malignant melanoma in her legs, the naturopath is now suffering from a possible metastasis of the cancer in her chest area and a stricture of the esophagus. "The obvious question," said the doctor, "is whether the esophageal stricture is related to the metastic lesion." Judge Bryson heard the last act out and then ordered Mrs. Bush to surrender to the sheriff on the following Monday for the trip to Salem. "I'll do my time like a squatting duck," Mrs. Bush told friends outside the courtroom. Any further move, apparently, will be a matter for the governor. Surely, he will be asked to consider whether any of the usual motives of incarceration will be served by the imprisonment of a woman gravely ill with cancer in the evening of her life. Rehabilitation? (Apparently not.) Example? (For Whom?) Protection of the public? (There is no evidence that any of Ruth Barnett Bush's patients were ever solicited, there is no sign that any of the thousands of women who asked for her services were ever charged with anything.) As the law stands—a law first formulated many years ago in a less-enlightened age—Ruth Barnett Bush is a felon. Here advanced years and deteriorating physical condition should have little or nothing to do with her serving her sentence. And yet, her confinement is sure to lie heavily on the conscience of a great many citizens. As her lawyer told Judge

Bryson at her hearing: "We are all a bunch of hypocrites."— Doug
Baker, February 1, 1968

THEY WEEP ON MY DOORSTEEP

CHAPTER ONE

Pregnant.

The word is alive with many meanings.

To know you are pregnant can fill your cup with joy. And to know that another life quickens in your womb can, in different circumstances, fill your heart with anguish and dread.

I know, because I have known both kinds of pregnancies.

In my 74 years of living, I have learned to keep many secrets. And I have learned to keep them well.

But I have lived too long to keep my own, personal secrets. The evening of life is a good time for reflection and for confession. So, I am going to tell you something which for most of my long, full life I never told to mother, father, husband, or even to closest friend:

The first abortion of which I ever had any experience was my own.

It was a long time ago, but a woman does not forget details of such an experience. His name was Frank. It all began casually enough, in the same way as half a dozen other dates except, perhaps, for one thing. Frank was older. He was 19 and I, 16. He was tall, energetic, full of talk about his future as an engineer, hinting at his prowess as a "ladies' man." And he was so handsome.

What more shall I try to recall? In the years since I first realized I was pregnant without being married, I have talked with and helped hundreds of girls who have had the same experience. With each it was much the same—a devastating, almost unbelievable nightmare of doubt and fear. With each it was her trouble and hers alone. Always there was the wrench in talking with these girls, I could not help but remember my own feelings long ago.

As I look back, I wonder what I saw in Frank. He was neither romantic, nor a rogue. Just an average youth, careless, thoughtless, ignorant perhaps; but so was I. I cannot, now, hold him to blame for what happened. But at the time, I did.

When I told him of my pregnancy, he was sympathetic at first, then resentful. He was not to blame, he said. What kind of a little fool had I been to be so careless?

"What are you bawling about? You can do something about it," he said.

When I tearfully asked him what and how and where, he shouted, "How should I know? That's for you to find out. You got yourself that way, now get yourself out of it." Seeing the look of amazement on my face, he added a thrust that I've heard second-hand a thousand times since. "How do I know I'm responsible anyways? You've been going around with other guys." I was too stunned to reply. He turned and hurried away. I never saw him again.

In the years that followed, I have observed many "Franks." Some of them came to my waiting room—as a general rule, unwillingly—accompanying their partners-in-trouble. Others, who had fled, as my Frank had, were described in familiar detail. For years I hated Frank. So it was no surprise to me to find many of my patients had the same implacable hatred for the man responsible. I did not blame them, but would often try, sometimes successfully, to talk them into a reconciliation—indeed, sometimes, marriage.

In my own case, there were plenty of worries besides the boy's irresponsibility. I became ill and lost weight rapidly. Morning nausea was a double problem—suffering through it and trying to keep mother from guessing its cause. Fortunately for both of us, she did not suspect pregnancy. Eventually, she diagnosed my illness as possibly being due to a malfunctioning appendix. She wanted me to consult our family physician, the last person I cared to see. I managed to avoid this confrontation. I knew, in a vague sort of way, that there were doctors in Portland who could have "done something" for a fee, but I had no idea how to find one. I did not know the word, abortion, nor what it was a doctor did. Nor did I have the faintest notion of what the cost would be, let alone how I could pay for it.

When I began making the notes for this book, a friend with whom I discussed the project asked me if my own pregnancy as a young girl had had anything to do with my becoming an abortionist and making it my life's work. The question was so naïve, it took me a bit aback. "It had everything to do with it," I answered.

After nearly half a century of helping girls and women in trouble, I have no doubts that at all about why I first became interested in the career that has brought me so much joy along with a full measure of grief.

But at the time of my own little tragedy I had no idea that my admiration for the man who helped me and others like him would lead me to my life's vocation.

And I had no idea then that I would ever share my secret for all to read. I have so often told my adorable granddaughter. "A still tongue makes a wise brain."

As she, along with you, reads this book, she will understand why my time for such secrets is past.

CHAPTER TWO

I was in high school when Dad decided to move his family from Hood River, a small town in Western Oregon, to Portland. I can't recall what prompted his decision, but I was all for it. I had been to the big city several times with Dad, but only for brief visits. Today, the drive from Hood River to Portland can be made easily in two hours. Then it was an all-day trip, generally by boat.

My childhood goes all but unmentioned in these memoirs. Dad was a grocer in Hood River and I was born over the grocery store. My brother, sister and I did a lot of riding, a lot of fishing. Nothing about my childhood is particularly memorable. It was as smooth as glass.

Now, I was to become an actual part of the city, and I could swing onto street cars with nonchalance. I must admit I spent more time daydreaming than assisting with the necessary moving preparations—the packing of chinaware, crating of furniture, rolling and wrapping of rugs and other chores.

Our first home in Portland, though not as large as the one in Hood River, was comfortable and, for those days, quite modern. Mother was always a good housekeeper, although she detested household duties, and Dad was a good provider. Consequently, our home life was not greatly affected by the move. But my transition from town to city girl did not go as I had planned so confidently. Without doubt, I was a pretty brash kid. I do not believe there was any meanness, or even cockiness behind it. It was only that I was used to knowing everyone and having everyone know me. In Hood River we said "hello" to both friends and strangers. In Portland, people were aloof. Where I started attending Washington High School, I ran into several pointed rebuffs. Adjusting as soon as I did, was in part due to buoyancy of spirt and in part to the instinctive kindness of Oregonians, country or city.

Many newcomers to Oregon have been perplexed by the reserve of the Oregonian. I think this could be a hold-over from the many New Englanders who pioneered the Pacific Northwest. But underneath the first layer of reserve was a core of true friendliness. This I firmly believe, in spite of the heartaches and vilification I have known these past years—one of the few things my mother had not prepared me for.

My mother was a lovely person. She was an excellent though reserved hostess when she had to be. When Dad brought home a business associate, without advance warning, Mother would be charming in spite of the fact Dad's guests were sometimes rather unusual. But Mother could get along without guests, expected or unexpected. She was content to live quietly in her own sphere. In Hood River she took part in a church club and sewing circle but, as far as I can remember, she never belonged to such a group after our move to Portland.

Mother loved her children—I had a sister and a brother—but never seemed particularly interested in their activities. I don't mean that she was not interested in our welfare. Far from it. A skinned knee received more attention than did a meningitis patient at John Hopkins Hospital. Every stray dog and cat in the neighborhood knew her ministrations. Yet, she never got around to discussing the birds and the bees with my sister, or with me. We had to learn about such things the hard way. Nor, so far as I can recall, did she offer advice of any when we grew old enough to think of careers. She lived her life in the center of the hurricane, never rebelling but never coming quite to terms with life. Years later, when the family home became my home and responsibilities all mine, she accepted the situation with the same calm she used to display when I would take over the cooking of Sunday's dinner to avoid going to church.

The sprint I called it quits at Washington High School found me with too much free time. Summer vacations in Hood River meant three months of fishing, hunting and camping. Now, living in Portland, and with no definite plans to go back to school in the fall, I could not resign myself to being idle. Mother, characteristically, offered no advice. Dad, busy with his business problems, still thought of me as his little girl. When one evening after supper, I told him I was going to find a job, he was mildly amused.

"Well, Ruthie, that's fine," he said. "What are you going to be– the world's roller-skating champion?" I had been on a racing team at Hood River, an interest from which he/ derived some kind of merriment. He chuckled and picked up his newspaper.

His condensation made me rash. "I'll show you," I said. "I'll be working before the end of the week." And I was. But it was pure luck that got me a job as a dental assistant. Well, "dental assistant" may be a blown-up title for the job. But I did go to work in a dentist office.

The next morning I went downtown with my cousin, Mary. She was on her way to the dentist and I to look for work of any kind. I tried the employment office of the city's largest department store and quickly worked my way down through a number of small, neighboring shops. But I was too young and inexperienced, or no help was wanted. Job hunting that morning ended earlier than I had expected.

I went back to the dentist's office to meet my cousin. Her coat was hanging in the empty reception room but there was no one around. While I waited, the telephone began ringing. It rang and rang and I couldn't resist picking up the receiver. Before I could say "hello," the dentist came rushing out of his inner office and snatched the telephone. I stood there, feeling silly, while he completed his conversation. When he had finished, he seemed to see me for the first time.

"Where's Mabel"? he demanded. I wasn't sure who he meant, but it was obvious he was angry. I told him I was waiting for Mary and he growled something about it being "no way to run a dentist's office." I shook my head sympathetically. I learned, later, that Dr. Earl McFarland was an excitable and irritable man. I also learned that he was a persistent though discreet wolf —his discretion dictated by fear of his good-sized wife. But at the moment I saw only a vacant job. I thought "Mabel" was very foolish to have left her desk.

"Dr. McFarland," I suggested, "if you're thinking of firing your receptionist, why not give me the job? I'm right here and I can start right now." He didn't notice the quaver in my voice. He stopped fidgeting and looked me up and down.

"All right," he said, "sit down and go to work. Just answer the phone and make appointments in that book. Tell callers I'm not in whenever you hear me shut the bolt to my office door. Nine to five. Saturday's included. Fifty dollars a month. Fifteen minutes for lunch. Better bring it with you. Right?"

"Right", I answered. Finding my first job was really a simple matter after all. By the time Cousin Mary was finished in the dentist's chair, I was busy at my desk. She gaped in surprise. I was a model of efficiency.

"When is your next appointment?" I asked, as professionally as I could, and we both laughed.

I worked for Dr. McFarland for almost a year. The first few months were rather exciting. It wasn't long before I was assisting the dentist in a minor way—standing by with a glass water or selecting and sterilizing instruments. I was soon earning the fifty dollars a month, but he never volunteered a raise and I never thought of asking for one. In fact, I was pretty well off with my salary. My dresses were simple and inexpensive. Shoes, stockings and underclothes, in those days, were cheap. And there was no income tax.

I suppose that to this point in my life I could be described as a typical small-town girl come to the city. My family was what we called an "average" family. My upbringing, by Presbyterian parents, had been God-fearing if not overly religious. My folks were honest and hard-working and, as their daughter, I was imbued with these ordinary virtues. I worked at my job and tried to learn. When I began to menstruate, I vowed that I would keep myself clean for the man I would eventually fall in love with and marry. I was not a prig or prude. I was a normal young girl, with a normal young girl's curiosity.

My social life, however, was changing during those first few months as a dental assistant. There were male admirers. For a while, more through luck than sense and knowledge, I skirted a number of the usual pitfalls. I learned some of the fundamental facts of life in the usual, haphazard way. I knew, for instance, that a casual sweetheart's kiss did not mean I would have a baby. But I did not know how easily it could become the prologue for one. That lesson I learned when the Big Romance I've already described came into my life.

When I realized that I was pregnant, that the boy responsible for my pregnancy was of no help to me, I thought vaguely of suicide, of hurling myself from the office window of the deep, cold waters of the Willamette River under the Morrison Bridge and of the vials of medicine in the office with the red letters spelling POISON.

I know that it sounds like a line from a cheap novel to say that when things look blackest, help comes from an unexpected sources. But life, more often than not, follow the patterns of cheap fiction. As so it was with me. The help I got was from a most unlikely person—a prostitute.

Jane Allen was a patient of Dr. McFarland. I assumed she was the wife or, possibly the daughter, of a well-to-do businessman. She was always smartly dressed, and her make-up and hair-do were flawless. I was a bit envious of her easy and seemingly sheltered life.

One afternoon, coming from the dentist's chair, she used my desk phone to make an appointment, then sat down to smoke a cigarette. Quickly, she dropped her pose of quiet dignity, became chatty, informal and interesting. Once past the initial shock of learning her true profession, I was fascinated by her stories. And I began to see a possible, though desperate, solution to my problem. I must have betrayed myself because, in the middle of a rather involved story about a church deacon who had tried to stop payment on a personal service check, she stopped abruptly.

"What's wrong, dearie?" she asked. "You look upset. You think all preachers are monks?"

"I was wondering," I said hesitantly, "what you do if you become pregnant?"

She looked at me sharply, then laughed. "Why you poor little chick," she said.

I tried a naïve deception, saying I was merely curious. "Someone I know…" I started to say. She chuckled and her laughter was brittle. Lighting another cigarette, she said matter-of-factly:

"I did get caught once, when I was about your age. Just about went nuts for a while until I got hold of old Dr.Watts. He has his office in the Oregonian Building."

I like to think of Dr. George Watts as I saw him that first afternoon, rather than in later years when illness and worry had taken their toll of his appearance if not his spirits. He was, then, in his early fifties. His high-domed forehead and white hair were imposing. Benevolence, kindliness and charm were his most apparent qualities. A motion picture producer would have cast him in the role of a kindly old family practitioner. He had a leisurely manner, as though I was the only patient in the world. Later, I learned that he had a large practice and his time was in constant demand.

Dr. Watts' had been a highly-skilled physician and surgeon with a general practice in the city's leading hospitals. His change to abortion surgery—at first occasionally, and then exclusively—was prompted by a desire to be of help to woebegone women.

I have had the same desire throughout my life, to be of service, and much of the credit must go to Dr. Watts and, later, to another man, Dr. Ed Stewart.

Dr. Watts' gentle voice and a sympathetic manner made it easy for me to talk at last. I told him—a stranger only a few minutes before—what I did not dare reveal to anyone else, even my mother. I was not embarrassed. I did not cry, nor become frightened when he led me to his surgery for an examination. Here, as in his consulting room, I was impressed with not only the antiseptic cleanliness but the wholesome purity that stems from plenty of hot water and soap suds. His instruments gleamed in sterilized precision. His examination was swift but thorough, gentle but firm. His very sureness instilled confidence.

Back in his office, Dr. Watts made steeples out of his strong well-formed hands. "Ruth," he said, "you've almost waited too long. But you can still be helped." He paused. "Have you got $85 dollars, or can you get hold of $85 by, say, next Saturday?" He seemed almost apologetic in having to mention money, a trait he never overcame.

I said I would have the money and be in his office at 2 p.m. Saturday. I had no idea where I was going to obtain such a large sum but was determined to get it somehow. I pawned couple of high school fraternity pins, did some fast-talking to a cousin about some mythical overdue payments to a book salesman, and bit by bit, put together the $85.

My abortion was almost an anticlimax. Dr. Watts performed it smoothly and painlessly. I began regaining my health at once. Soon, I was putting on weight. Buoyantly, I faced life, happy in the knowledge that my "mistake," which once seemed so terrifying, was now a closed book.

Who had been hurt by this supposedly illegal operation? Society? My perturbation had not disturbed a solitary friend, relative or Portland Citizen.

Myself? I suffered no disturbing effects. If anything, I became healthier. Certainly, the procreative functions were in no way altered, because, later, I became the mother of a healthy child, delivered under normal circumstances. I was relieved of an exaggerated burden of apprehension and terror, instead of undergoing the trauma that inevitably comes to a young, unmarried girl who gives birth to an illegitimate child.

Dr. Watts? Hardly. He performed a minor surgical operation successfully, knowing that he had been instrumental in relieving the mental disquietude of a girl in trouble. And he had been paid for his services.

One of the mankind's man-made laws had been thwarted. But I was unable to perceive any crime in what either I or the doctor had done. Today, I am 58 years older and, presumably a great deal wiser. But I still cannot see the wrong in abortion.

CHAPTER THREE

Romance came early into my life again less than a year after my abortion. I was still working in the dentist's office where my recovery, a few months before, had mystified and intrigued my boss. He came bolder in his advances, but I knew how to fend them off. He saved his wounded ego by demanding extra work and criticizing the way I did it. The job was becoming onerous. I determined to look for a change and found it—by getting married.

It would not be accurate to say I married Harry Cohen to get out of the dentist's office. I was sincerely fond of Harry. And while that may not be the same as love, I thought it was—or would, eventually, become love.

At my wedding reception at the old Oregon Grill in 1913 I met a woman who was to be a great influence in my life. She was Dr. Alys Griff, a physician and surgeon of considerable prominence. As Dr. Alys Abigail Bixby, she had been graduated from the University of Oregon Medical School in 1902, becoming one of the earlier women physicians in the North-west.

Dr. Griff was married to Floyd Griff, Harry's best man for the wedding and it was Alys who gave my reception at the cabaret where Trader Vic's Restaurant is located nowadays. I was immediately taken with Alys. There were more beautiful women at the reception, but there was something in Dr. Griff's bearing, a vivaciousness she possessed in spite of being a heavy-set woman, which set her apart from others of her sex. Her severe brown suit was expensive and perfectly tailored. She handled herself with charm and confidence in a room crowded with happy, relaxed, laughing people. I was most impressed with her eyes. They were the first cold, brown eyes I had ever seen.

Soon after our marriage, Harry and I moved to Seattle. He was the sales representative in the Northwest for Can't-Bust-'Em overalls and Argonaut work shirts. We settle down to a fairly bourgeois mode of living.

I found myself making frequent trips to Portland, ostensibly to see Mother and Dad. Actually, I spent most of the time during my visits to Oregon with Dr. Griff.

I was still a youngish thing and the doctor was an idol of sorts. In turn, she seemed to like my company. She would take me along on her house calls and to Good Samaritan Hospital where we would visit the maternity wards. I would sit up in the gallery above the operating room and watch her perform appendectomies, hysterectomies and Caesareans. She was a jolly, wonderful woman and I enjoyed her company.

She had been specializing in diseases of women but so many women were coming to her for abortions that she had less and less time for the rest of her practice. Shortly after my marriage to Cohen, she had been divorced from Floyd and was living alone in the Oregon Hotel. After her day's work we would sit for hours in her suite and talk. Rather she would talk, and I would listen. These conversations, all dealing with her work, increasingly stimulated by my interest in the medical matters, particularly when we discussed abortions, for, from the time of my own abortion, my interest in this operation had grown. It seemed to me the most wonderful work in the world. The sub-conscious urge to make this my life's work must have been growing fast, although I did not realize it. The thought that I might actually be of help to women in this way began to obsess me.

Each time I would return to Seattle during those five years my marriage lasted, I would notice a growing rift with my husband. He spent most of his time on the road with his sales work or playing interminable pinochle games with his friends. So our married life continue until my baby was born.

The arrival of baby Margaret created intense excitement in

my in-law's house. Even Harry became, for a while, a family man, handing out the traditional cigars and playing the proud father with typical aplomb.

But this phase passed quickly. When he first began neglecting me, I was hurt and humiliated. After Margaret's birth, I became indifferent to him. I permitted things to drift for almost two years. Inevitably, the thin pretense of being married could no longer be maintained. I sued for divorce. Harry did not contest the suit and agreed to pay me a small monthly allowance.

Margaret and I returned to Portland, to my old room at Mother's, and I did some thinking about the future. I did not appear too rosy. I had a two-and-a-half-year-old child, a mother and father growing older, a small alimony and little savings. What I needed was a job. But what kind of job? What was I best fitted for? The only work I had done was in a dentist's office, so I turned my planning to that experience.

My brother commanding office of the Student Army Training Corps at Reed College and North Pacific Dental Collage. I decided to enroll at North Pacific for a course in prophylaxis—the treatment of pyorrhea and scaling and cleaning of teeth. After six months I got a job with an advertising dentist with a big suite of offices in the Lafayette Building over Rich's Cigar Store. It was interesting work and the pay was fairly good for those days— $27.50 a week. I was managing as well. Life was serene and the future looked secure until one day the dentist told me the state legislature office had changed the dentistry laws and my diploma no longer covered the many additional subjects required for dental hygienists.

"And what does that mean?" I asked.

"That I must let you go," he frowned, "much as I hate to do it. You've done an excellent job." He got up from his desk, adding, "You'll want to go back to school anyways, to learn those new-fangled didoes. But see me when you finish."

I never saw the inside of a dental office again after that—except as a patient. My short career in dentistry ended before it really started. Going back to school for another three months to take additional subjects was out of the question. I had no savings and I had to earn some money for living expenses as quickly as possible.

I was changing from my dental assistant's uniform when I was called to the telephone. It was Dr. Griff, inviting me to dinner. I had not seen her in three months. Her clinic had been terribly busy. World War I had left many women with unwanted pregnancies. When I saw her, I was shocked at the change. It showed itself in little ways: she snapped at the waiter, abruptly terminated phone calls—things like that.

But she was cordial and pleasant to me and I still admire her, especially for the work she was doing. I told her about my enforced "retirement" from the dental profession. She told me about her clinic and how busy she was. All through dinner we must have been mulling over the same idea. By the time we got to the dessert one of us—I can't remember which—had broached the subject of my coming to work for her.

"I think you know I'm dedicated to my work," said Dr. Griff. "It demands dedication. And that can't be just a word. You've got to care, about the patient, about the work itself."

"I know", I answered. I did not tell her then, or even after, about my personal experience with abortion.

She lit a Chesterfield and sat, staring at the window, rolling the cigarette back and forth between her tobacco-stained fingers.

I watched her reflection in the restaurant window. Beyond it, I saw couples passing by, some laughing, some quarrelling, others silent. The street was more crowded than during any peace-time Saturday night. And there seemed to be more hysteria than real happiness.

"There's a great deal to learn," she said, after a while. "There is so much you don't know. You couldn't be of any help for quite some time." She looked at me with those cold brown eyes. "I wouldn't be able to pay you much."

"I don't care," I said. "I'll work for anything you say." I watched as she looked at me closely. "I learn quickly," I added

35

with confidence. Then, suddenly, I thrust out my hands palms up, saying, "And my hands are steady."

She looked at my hands and smiled. "Suppose I pay you fifty a week to start."

"Starting as of now!" I insisted.

And so, I began to learn the technique of abortion. And I began to learn many other things. I learned not to be shocked at the sordid, not to be surprised at the ludicrous. Rapidly, I learned that I must put aside a lot of youthful illusions.

After just a few weeks I was permitted to get the patients ready and to stand by Dr. Alys while she operated. As time went on, I assisted in difficult cases. Sometimes, Dr. Griff would become so nervous she would have to leave the patient before finishing the procedure. I would then complete surgery, a responsibility I was glad to assume.

During these years I became fully acquainted with the woes and ways of women in trouble. At the time I thought I would remember each case, but I find, now, I have forgotten most. I do not say that they were commonplace, because no pregnant woman's plight is commonplace, at least to herself. It was only a case of today's experience overshadowing yesterday's as tomorrows will erase today's.

Of course, random memories remain—incidents and sidelights on human nature more vivid than the clinical details. I remember looking over my desk one morning at a very pretty girl of about 19. She was dressed in a becoming, obviously new suit. Pinned to her lapel was a wedding corsage of forget-me-nots. She held back tears as I questioned her. I asked her if she was married and, "Does your husband know your coming here?"

"I don't know," she began, and the tears came. "I mean, I don't know if he's going to be my husband. We were to be married at noon, but he said to come here first."

This was an emergency—and a novel one. "Is your husband-to-be the father?" I asked. She said he was. "Then you have nothing to worry about," I assured her, and I called Dr. Griff.

After an hour with Dr. Griff, quite recovered and radiant instead of tearful, the bride was back in my office, asking to use the phone. She dialed a number and asked for "Edward." For a full minute she listened, and her face grew white. The she hung up without saying another word.

"What's the matter?" I asked. "Anything wrong?"

"Not a thing, not a thing," she said, "except, the marriage is cancelled. Edward left me standing at the altar, the sonofabitch.

CHAPTER FOUR

Those eleven years with Dr. Alys Bixby Griff began in the final year of the Great War and continued through most of the tumult of the Roaring Twenties.

For me, still a young woman, they were exciting years. Dr. Griff was a nervous woman but a jolly person with a great zest for life.

Nothing creates patients for an abortionist like a war with its whirlwind romances, hurried leave-takings and increased promiscuity. Patients came to Dr. Griff's offices in the Lafayette Building at S.W. 6th and Washington in a steady stream. At times, there were three or four girls waiting in the waiting room and another two or three on couches in the inside offices.

Our office hours in those days began at 11 a.m. and ended at four o'clock in the afternoon. But there was other work, too. Many a night I would go to one of the Japanese hotels or another and take care of some girl with a miscarriage.

We worked hard and we played hard. After work we would whoop it up until all hours of the morning.

We all lived in the old Oregon Hotel on those days. Dr. Griff had Rooms 225 and 226, beautifully furnished rooms on the second-floor right at S.W. Stark and Broadway. My room was 227 and Dr. Marie Equi, the famous Socialist, lived in 228.

Dr. Alys was a wonderful cook. She could go into the bathroom with just a breadboard and a chafing dish. She'd put the breadboard across the bathtub and a half hour later she'd come out of there with as fine a dinner you've ever seen.

Night after night, we'd go to parties. Those were Prohibition days and we'd drink all kinds of things. We used to drink from vats of homemade brew that were alive with gnats. We'd just ladle the beer right out of the vat with a big dipper and drink it. We had a Japanese janitor at the hotel and he could always get us a bottle of sake.

We'd go out to the roadhouses—Twelve Mile or the Clackamas Tavern. There were four or five wonderful roadhouses out on Linnton Road in those years. The doctor always had a big car, either a Winton or a Pierce Arrow. We had some great times. When you work hard, you appreciate the laughs, the big dinners and the booze.

There were so many funny things that happened in those days, it's not easy to remember them all. I remember one time a girl came to the office for an examination and Dr. Griff told her to get up on the operating table. The girl didn't know what position to assume.

"Just get up on the table in the same position you were in when this happened to you," said Dr. Griff.

"But I had my feet through the windshield," said the girl. We laughed over that one for years.

During those years in the Lafayette Building, Dr. Marie Equi was our office neighbor as well as our next-door-neighbor in the old Oregon Hotel. She and Dr. Alys were close friends, and I came to know her in that way.

Mary Equi—we always called her "Mary," not Marie—was a "Wobbly," a member of the International Workers of the World and a dedicated Socialist with a raft of friends among working men. She also numbered some of the greats of the earth among her acquaintances. I recall Margaret Sanger, the courageous woman who pioneered birth control, coming to see her. Another friend of hers, as I remember, was Eamon de Valera, the fiery New York-born revolutionary who became president, and later prime minister, of Ireland.

Federal investigators used to come into the office and ask me about her business. I've always told them I knew her but knew nothing about her business. I've always been one to keep my nose out of matters that don't concern me, and I've never been a stool pigeon for anybody.

During World War I, Dr. Equi rode around town on the back end of a truck, speaking out against the war and urging men not to enlist in the army. She was beaten by a mob and arrested under the Espionage Act.

She appealed her conviction all the way to the Supreme Court, but finally went to San Quentin. President Woodrow Wilson had reduced her three-year sentence to a year and a day and she was in the federal prison for 10 months.

From what I heard, Dr. Equi was a terrible inmate, always rebelling against the rules. Dr. Griff and I took care of a lot of her patients for her while she was in the federal penitentiary. I remember that first Christmas she was there she wrote and asked me to buy Christmas presents for about 20 of the other women prisoners. I bought mostly things for them to embroider and a lot of stockings.

After Dr. Equi was released from prison, she continued to do nice things for the inmates there, sending turkeys for the Christmas along with candy and other things. She continued for some years to be featured in the newspapers. In 1927 she was arrested at the Heilig Theater during a performance of "Mitzi." They charged her with being "drunk and disorderedly." I never understood the drunk part of the charge because she certainly wasn't a drinking woman. She was a very heavy smoker and her hands were always black from cigarette tar. And at the time of the Heilig arrest she said she was merely protesting the showing of the play which she said was "risqué." The court finally issued an order restraining her from ever re-entering the Heilig.

I once wrote a little song about Dr. Equi. The lyric went like this"

"Mary was the queen of the Bolsheviks.
Everywhere she went her name was known.
Blue eyes, hair the color of gold
And disposition strictly all her own.
She'd stand atop a soapbox,
A red flag in her hand,

She'd teach democracy throughout the land.
She always caught nickels and dimes
And gave the boys a cheer,
And all at once the boys began to sing,
'Let Mary alone, alone, alone,
Let Mary alone, Uncle Sam...
...Keep her out of the pen...'"

On September 15, 1919, which was 13 months before Dr. Equi went to jail, President Wilson and Mrs. Wilson visited Portland. President Wilson was touring the United States in his campaign to win the people to his idea of a League of Nations.

I remember the parade down Broadway distinctly. Dr. Alys and I had an excellent view of the second floor of the old Oregon Hotel. We were wearing our kimonos and Dr. Equi, two windows away from us, was in her pajamas with a suit coat over the top of them. I remember it so well, because Dr. Equi shouted to Dr. Griff when the Wilson came by, "Mrs. Wilson looks like you, Al'." There was a resemblance and it was accentuated because Mrs. Wilson was wearing a big floppy hat and Dr. Griff always wore floppy hats.

But that afternoon when I bought a copy of the Portland Telegram, there was a story which said, "Among the witnesses to the parade was Dr. Marie Equi who stood at the curb in a little, chic blue suit, and said, in a quavering voice, 'I wanted to see him,' and then sped on and was lost in the crowd."

From that time on, I've never really believed a newspaper version of anything.

CHAPTER FIVE

My break-up with Dr. Griff came slowly. It is never easy to break with someone you have admired with that kind of blind allegiance of which only the young are capable.

However, over the years I came to realize that Dr. Griff, while a skilled and competent surgeon, was far from being the paragon of perfection I had once believed her to be. Her operation techniques lacked the true professionalism I knew possessed by others. She lacked genuine self-confidence and she became increasingly fretful about her patients, increasingly concerned about her responsibility to them and more and more worried about each operation. More and more, she was leaving the difficult cases to me.

Today, with the equanimity that comes from hindsight, I can look back and analyze the factors which led to my leaving. There were two sore spots that had been festering.

One of these were purely something that grew out of our intimacy. About 1924, Dr. Alys became involved with a character who passed himself off as a "Bohemian nobleman." He was taking her for everything he could get. She gave him an expensive diamond ring and a costly automobile. She even entrusted him with $24,000 which he was supposed to use to buy a home for when they were married. She was such a fool about it all that it came as a rude awakening to her to learn that her "Bohemian nobleman with vast European estates" was really an already married man. I became very angry with her and we quarreled bitterly. That quarrel was never completed healed.

From that time on, our relationship deteriorated on another level. She was becoming more and more nervous in handling patients. To be fair, it must be remembered that she was under a terrific strain and her health was beginning to fail. And I would be less than honest if I did not concede that my marriage in 1920 to Paul Barnett, an insurance adjuster, was a little rocky (it finally collapsed after nine years, a victim of many friendships of which Paul grew increasingly intolerant) and imposed another strain of friendship with Alys.

But, inevitably, there came a day when she flared up in a burst of temper over a minor misunderstanding. The temper tantrum led to hysterics. I quit my job. And I quit it cold.

For a brief time after leaving Dr. Griff, I tried my hand in the beauty business. I had a friend named Bonnie who had a darling little beauty salon across from the Paramount Theater. She'd lost interest in it, so I bought it from her. I believe I gave her $1,800. The whole experiment lasted about six months.

One of the problems with the shop was that it had more male customers than women. They'd come in for a manicure and they'd get my knee between their legs and squeeze it. It was obvious that they were more interested in what was under the table than what was above. I soon tired of all that. I gave the shop back to Bonnie and I didn't even ask her to return my money.

I went to the Broadway Building and sought out Dr. George Watts, my benefactor of nearly 20 years before. "I don't know," he said. "I've never had a nurse in my life."

"Well you need one," I said. "Just look at your office. Look at those diplomas on the wall. Why not some pretty pictures? Look at that old roll-top desk and how drab everything is."

I told Dr. Watts that I had to work. My marriage to Paul Barnett of a few years before was on the rocks and we had separated. My daughter was in boarding school.

"You just have to hire me," I said. "I can fix this office up and I can help you with your patients. You don't want the job of telling women how to take care of themselves after they go home from here and that sort of thing. You need a nurse to take care of them."

He asked me when I wanted to go to work and I told him I'd start that very day. I had a friend who needed an abortion and I wanted to bring her in so he could take care of her. When I look back at it, it wasn't so much his hiring me, as my just not leaving the office. But after a while, he said, "Well, all right, Ruth."

Stippling paint was something new then, and I got the house man to paint all the walls and I stippled them with a big sponge. I brought down the drapes from my sunroom at home and made the doctor go out and pick out a beautiful, flat-top desk.

In the early days of that three years with Dr. Watts I had little to do with the actual operations. I answered the phone, made appointments, kept charge of the cash and paid the bills. Soon, I was interviewing patients, preparing them for surgery, sterilizing the instruments and keeping them in order.

After a time, he began instructing me in the painstaking details of his technique. Both his instruments and his methods were far superior to Dr. Griff's. The instruments were solid bronze and custom made for him. You can't get instruments like that nowadays. Unlike Dr. Griff and the gynecologists who do hospital abortions, he never used a dilator. And after working with him I never used a dilator, either.

He was an excellent teacher and I a willing pupil. I absorbed information like a sponge. I learned so quickly that one day he suggested I should enroll in a college to earn a license as a naturopathic physician. This would give me the right to practice as Dr. Ruth Barnett.

Dr. Watts had two reasons for wanting me to get a license as a naturopath. First, he recognized my ability. He believed in my sincerity to help women by means of abortion. But, to do this minor surgery I must have proper credentials. Certainly, my training under Dr. Griff and himself had qualified me to perform abortions with as much skill as most medical school graduates. But according to the law that was insufficient. Text-book learning was required.

His second reason was that eventually he would retire, and I might take over his practice.

A naturopathy course, in those days, required only 27 months of study and it was possible to attend night classes and continue working days at the clinic. Dr. Watts said he would advance the necessary tuition.

Pacific States Chiropractic College was a modest, two-story building at the corner of Grand Avenue and Burnside in downtown Portland. There was no campus, no frills. The instructors were competent and matter-of-fact. Two of them had offices in the Broadway Building and they gave me a great deal of tutoring outside of school hours. I used to sit in the office with a pathology book when there weren't many patients. They gave me some credit for the time I had spent at North Pacific Dental College and I wasn't required to go the full 27 months.

But I studied a great deal and learned a lot. I took courses in anatomy, physiology, histology and chemistry. When they gave the courses in chiropractic, I looked out the window. I wasn't interested in that.

Naturopathy, to over-simplify, is concerned with restoring health by assisting the body's own health-restoring potential. It is licensed and widely accepted throughout the United States and elsewhere. The naturopath is permitted to perform minor surgery—surgery where entry is made through a natural body opening. I was within a month of graduation and getting my diploma when I came suddenly to another of those abrupt turning points in my life.

Dr. Watts was not the only abortionist practicing in the Broadway Building. Dr. Maude K. Van Alstyne, a stocky woman of about sixty, had a small suite off of offices down the hall. She was dour and aloof, barely nodded when we encountered each other. I met her receptionist, Beatrice, that fateful day. She told me Dr. Van Alstyne was talking of retiring.

"Do you think she'd sell her clinic?" I asked.

"I think so," Beatrice replied.

"I'll buy it," I said, bursting with confidence.

I called on Dr. Van Alstyne the next day. She acknowledged she was thinking of retiring. But she would not sell to a man—

she did not approve of male abortionists—but she might consider selling to me. Money seemed to be the biggest obstacle.

"How much can you raise?" she asked.

"Two thousand dollars—for a down payment," I said, naming
a figure I grabbed out of the air. "The balance to be paid in
monthly instalments."

"All right," Dr. Van Alstyne agreed. "I'll have the necessary
papers for your signatures tomorrow."

"I'll be here at noon," I said.

I scurried about to raise the money. Beatrice had told me she
would stay on as my receptionist/ She did even better than that.
She lent me $500. I took my savings and made a loan against
my salary. There, I went to the kindest and most generous man I
knew.

"Dr. Watts," I said. "I need your help."

He smiled, "Tell me about it."

I explained what I had done and what I intended to do. The
Van Alstyne Clinic was his competition. It was the measure of
the man that he did not mention this. "You'll need more money
than you think," he said. "There'll be office rent, lights, phone,
laundry and such. The money can be managed easily enough—
I'll be glad to let you have it. But, Ruth, it seems to me you're
overlooking a pretty important item."

"I've no license—is that what you mean?"

"Exactly," he said. "If you have to lock the door even for a
couple of months, your practice would be down to nothing."

"I have no intention of locking the door," I said.

"But you can't operate alone, Ruth."

"No, but you can."

"Well—you seem to have it all planned. Suppose you tell me
where I come in."

My diploma and license were scarcely a month away, I added.
I should have waited until the license was in my hand before I
talked to Dr. Van Alstyne, but she might have sold to someone
else. The matter of the license was not important as long as Dr.
Van Alstyne's—my clinic—was only a few steps from Dr. Watts'

and if he did the surgery, I could prepare the patients. He could come down the hall to my clinic—how I loved those words—where an operating room and sterile gloves and his instruments would be ready for him.

"You'll explain this to the patients?" he inquired.

"Yes," I said, and Dr. Watts agreed.

Dr. Van Alstyne and her lawyer were waiting for me at the noon. The papers were signed, the money paid. Then she donned her hat and walked out, without a backward look. I sat down at her desk—now my desk.

After years of working for other people, I finally had my own clinic. Beatrice stayed on as a receptionist. Each patient was told why Dr. Watts would perform the actual surgery. We had a buzzer rigged up and when they were all ready for his ministrations, we would sound the buzzer and he'd come down the hall. No one objected to the odd arrangement which continued until I received my license.

I rarely saw Dr. Watts after I took over for my own surgery. Sometimes I operated on women who had been his patients, but I attributed this either to a normal shift or, perhaps, to the fact that women in distress often feel more at ease with another woman. But soon Beatrice, at the reception desk heard differently.

"He's retiring, or he's sick," she said. "He's sending his patients to you."

"I'll look into it," I said, a bit puzzled.

I went down the hall to Dr. Watts' office and found him in his surgery, packing his instruments for shipment.

Dr. Watts, it seemed, was planning to open a clinic in Los Angeles, the largest and finest anywhere, in partnership with Reg Rankin, a self-proclaimed humanitarian who believed every woman had the right to an abortion. This was to be the first step in a gigantic scheme. Dr. Watts was to train other doctors recruited by Rankin and instruct them in his highly-developed abortion technique. As fast as these men and women became proficient, they would staff other Rankin clinics in other California cities until there was a chain of abortion offices from the Mexican border to the Oregon line.

I heard the details. "Rankin has big ideas," I said.

"He's a fine fellow, Ruth."

"Undoubtedly," I said. "But I'd do a lot of looking before I leaped, if I were you. I'd check the California law, and investigate Rankin, too."

"There's nothing to worry about, Ruth."

Later that day when Watts came to say good-bye he brought Red Rankin to my office. He was a glib, smoothly aggressive, white-maned man of forty-odd. He may have been a humanitarian, but his talk was mainly of money. I did not like him.

"Dr. Watts tells me you've the finest touch of anyone he knows," was his gambit. "We want you in our organization as soon as we begin to expand. We'll open a clinic for you that will make this one look like a broom closet."

"I'm very happy here," I said.

"You'll change your mind," Watts said.

I was sorry to see him go. He was a dedicated doctor as well as a good friend to me and I did not like his new associate.

I could see trouble ahead for that sweet old man.

CHAPTER SIX

Where there had been three clinics in the Broadway Building —Watts', Van Alstyne's (now mine) and Dr. Ed Stewart's—there were now two.

Dr. Steward, a soft-spoken and pleasant man, a skilled surgeon who also had been trained by Watts in abortion technique, was not in good health. He had coronary trouble. His office was two floors above mine, much older, far larger, the most elaborate on the Pacific coast. He had had all the business he could handle before Watts left for California. Thus, most of the patients who would have gone to Dr. Watts, came to me. It was not a question of real competition. Dr. Steward and I were very friendly. There was plenty of work for both of us.

And I loved it. I was young and strong and my health was good. I liked the income, naturally. But most of all, I liked what I was doing. In spite of my patients' tears and anguish, I toiled in a happy climate, because here, in my surgery, came the end of tears and anguish.

Each patient had made her personal decision before she came, had weighed the arguments pro and con before she walked through my door. And each found of her own free will good and sufficient reason for an abortion. I was the instrument, the means by which it was accomplished, quickly, safely and without pain. I saw those tears dried and those smiles appear; those who had feared disgrace, walk out of the office with heads held high, unafraid to face the world.

Occasionally I heard news of Dr. Watts. Some years later during a trip to Los Angeles, I went to see him. Visiting royalty could not have had a more enthusiastic reception. He took me on a tour of his clinic, saying, "Here's Ruth!" as if I were someone special.

The setting lived up to its advance billing, in size at least. It was well staffed and very busy. There were gleaming surgeries, consultation, examination and recovery rooms. We went into his office and a nurse brought us tea.

"Well?" he said. "What do you think?"

"You must be doing very well," I said.

He glowed as he quoted figures. The daily patient load was staggering. Already, a number of doctors had been trained and branches opened in other cities. The Rankin plan for establishing a chain of abortion offices was processing famously.

"There's a place here for you," he said. "Why don't you change your mind and join us, Ruth?"

I agreed to think about it, but it was pure evasion. My decision had already been made. I considered that running my own clinic was too fulfilling an experience to be given up lightly. I had my independence. Besides, the Rankin-type operation was too large and impersonal. The individual was lost in the endless flow of patients. There was no feeling of warmth or sympathy. Efficiency was the keyword. And there seemed to be an over-riding, over-concern with money.

Rankin had overlooked nothing. At first, patients with lean purses had been sent away to raise the fee, in cash. When many of them said, later, that they had obtained the money for loan companies, Rankin decided there was an additional mine to be worked. He opened a loan office, catering to his clients.

"Keep in touch," said Dr. Watts as we said our adieux. "Write often," I said.

I did write to him, sporadically. Each letter brought a reply urging me to participate in the clinic. Much as I admired Dr. Watts, I had no intention of working in an organization where policies were dictated by an entrepreneur such as Rankin.

As the years went by, it appeared that my premonitions about Rankin's enterprise and old Dr. Watts becoming involved in something that would make him trouble were baseless. It was a decade or more before I saw my fears realized.

Distressing rumors came first, emanating from Los Angeles. They were the first vague murmurings before the storm. One of my patients reported: "Something's going on down there." A letter from Dr. Watts said: "We've had visitors, Ruth. The federal government seems to be interested in us.: Then word came that the Rankin-Watts organization was in deep trouble; the Bureau of Internal Revenue had moved on them. "Awkward," Watts' next letter said, "but nothing to worry about. Reg tells me it will all be ironed out in a week or two."

The Rankin-Watts outfit had grown too fast, become too big. They made too much money and were vulnerable on many levels. Word of their tax troubles reached the newspapers and, soon, ministers in California were thundering about the monsters who ran the abortion chain. Next, the politically-ambitious district attorneys leaped into the fray. They must have long known of the chain's existence because no real effort had been made to hide the operation. Previous knowledge or not, the moralistic juggernaut was rolling now. Here was a crusade that would yield a harvest of headlines.

The parent office was raided, and Rankin, Watts, the doctors in training and nurses were jailed. Raid followed raid, as other district attorneys struck at the branch offices. When the crusade, Rankin, Watts and a number of their nurses and doctors were in San Quentin.

It was hard for me to imagine George Watts, the gentlest of men, wearing prison denim and living behind bars. He died there soon after and his body was shipped from San Quentin to Portland for private burial. None of his many friends was permitted to attend the services. Later, we drove out to the cemetery to put flowers on his grace and say a quiet good-bye to an old and dear friend.

Standing by his grave, feeling a chilly shudder go through me, I had another of my presentiments—that soon I, too, would become a victim of unreasoning prejudice.

CHAPTER SEVEN

The depression of the '30's was still with us when I bought Dr. Van Alstyne's clinic. People had stopped jumping out of windows and the apple salesmen had vanished from the street corners, but unemployment was still a staggering statistic. Money was hard to get and even harder to keep.

A beginning abortionist, like any fledgling medic, had to build a practice. I had by-passed that problem, in part, by purchasing a going practice. But that did not mean that all Dr. Van Alstyne's patients there their friends would flock to me. More important, it did not assure my obtaining any volume of referral work from the medical profession. That was something that I had to earn. As a result, there were many slack days when Beatrice and I would sit around waiting for the phone to ring or the door to open. And there were other days when we were so busy, we could not find time for luncheon—especially on the weekends.

Those who could not pay the full fee gave whatever they could. An abortionist's fees are based on a length-of-pregnancy scale. When I was with Dr. Griff she charged $25 for women who had missed only one period, $50 for those over their second period and $75 for more difficult cases. It is the same nowadays and there is a good reason for such a sliding scale. An early abortion is a relatively simple matter. In a more advanced pregnancy, there is always a chance of hemorrhage and this means a great deal more work and responsibility for the doctor.

In those depression days, some women paid nothing. And those who were more affluent were charged somewhat more than the usual fee. I make no apology for this practice. Medical clinics of all kinds are run on the same principles. I chose to charge off any deficit to the memory of a young, quondam dental assistant, who, long ago, needed help and found there were some people who cared. I never forgot my own experience and difficulty in raising the needed money.

Ours was strictly a cash business. A clinic of the traditional sort could send monthly statements, knowing that most of the patients would eventually pay their bills. We had to balance income against overhead daily. Too much charity work would not pay the overhead.

Sometimes, I found myself acting as a bill collector for my patients. There was Polly O'hara, for instance, a high school girl whose mother brought her to us and whose name I have changed. I heard Polly's story in the consultation room, and it was neither new nor startling. She was the oldest of five children. Her father was a construction engineer who had lost his job. A lengthy illness wiped out his savings. He had had to sell his home and move the family to a rented house in a poorer neighborhood.

Polly was rushed by a popular boy in her school class. His father owned one of Portland's better retail stores. The boy had a car and plenty of pocket money. At the time, he may have believed he was genuinely in love with Polly, or he may have pretended. But the inevitable happened and Polly became pregnant. When she revealed her situation, he wanted to have nothing more to do with her.

Polly told her mother, a use and sympathetic woman. The mistake had been made and she accepted it, not as a means of chastising her daughter but as a matter for consideration and decision. The next step, to her, was obvious. Abortion. But how to get the money. Fortunately, this was school vacation. Mrs. O'Hara took her five children with her to work in the berry and beans fields. Their small earnings were pooled. Then she brought the money to us.

"I know it's not enough," she said, "but it's all we have."

I told her, "Your daughter didn't get pregnant by herself. That boy certainly shared the responsibility. He shared the pleasure. He should share the costs."

"I know," she said, "but I talked to his mother and they won't help."

"Let me see what I can do."

I knew the boy's father by reputation. He was said to be an honest man, stiff-backed, proud and on the prudish side. He had a flaming temper and his verbal explosions were legendary in the retail business. I had a hunch the boy had not confided in him. This hunch was strengthened the next day when I phoned his mother and she agreed to come to my office with her son.

Junior was an uneasy lad, big of hand, big of foot, and red of face. If even half of what I heard of his father's temper were true, Junior would certainly be bearing some marks had his father learned of his escapade. The mother was expensively dressed and glacially calm. She had come, she said, to set me straight. She was not going to pay any part of that girl's operation. Her son may have had relations with Polly O'hara, but that did not make him responsible for her condition. After all, there were other boys in high school she told me archly.

"What about that, Junior?" I asked. "What's your story?"

"Well, I..."

"Polly says you were the first and only."

He blushed even redder until his face looked like a brick. "I- - - I guess I am," he stammered.

Junior's mother now made a long speech, shaking her finger at me. Her boy had been led astray. He was too innocent to realize that he had been duped—and on and on. I heard her out... the same old excuses and rationalization. One thing caught my attention, however. Her nail polish. It was the same shade of red as the berry stains on Mrs. O'Hara's hands.

When she finally finished, I said, "Perhaps I should discuss this matter with your husband."

I reached the telephone and began to dial. She hesitated only a moment, then opened her purse. She paid for the operation, the entire amount of $75. Then she left as grandly as she had entered. The boy seemed pleased, and I think, relieved at having met some measure of his responsibility. He looked back at me from the doorway, grinned and clasped his hands together over his head in the manner of a victorious prize-fighter.

I never saw the youth again, but some months later, while shopping, I met his parents formally. They were with a mutual friend. His mother looked frightened when she saw me. Her face was set in severe lines and she looked at me without recognition.

"We've already met," I said when we were introduced, "but for the life of me I can't remember where."

She extended her hand, squeezing my fingers as an expression of gratitude.

But it was not always that easy. There was the girl who could not seek help from the man involved because she did not know his name. "He wore a blue suit and drove a convertible," she said. "And he smelled so nice..." she added vaguely.

The bundle-from-heaven announcement often blights a budding romance. Yesterday all was undying love; today, he was important business in another town, and love boards the airplane with him. Stop worrying and everything will be all right, he says. And away he goes into the wild blue yonder.

When time makes a liar of him; when the weeks are measured by the tell-tale protuberance; and when she must write and tearfully ask for help, she will receive a curt letter of disavowal. Much has been said about the "Dear John" letters and the soul-searching effect they had on our men in uniform overseas. But as weapons of brutal ego-destruction, they can scarcely be compared to similar letters addressed to "Dear Jane."

I have seen many of these letters, too many. They come out of the purses of the despairing women in the consulting room, crumpled and stained by many distraught readings. "He was so nice, so kind and thoughtful." The wording varies, but the message seldom changes. He is sorry, but things are rugged for him, too. He had to buy new clothes and is fresh out of money. Or he has just been married and his wife would not like his sending money to another woman. He is sorry the letter is so brief, but he is a little rushed for time.

The fleetfooted bachelor who can pack and leave town in an instant is not the only one who is startled by unexpected fatherhood. There are solid citizens, pillars of the community, who become furious when the "office wife" breaks the headline news. The brush-offs vary in type. Sometimes they follow the pattern used by a prominent Portland businessman. He told each new secretary that his marriage had long ago gone stale and was dead. Divorce was imminent and would be forthcoming as soon as a few small details were ironed out. Meanwhile, why not make beautiful music together? Then, when the divorce comes through...

A tired, old pitch? Yes. But that pillar of the community sold it to several naïve girls I knew. It takes two to consort as well as tango. But there was no way for the new secretary to know that her boss was a philanderer. And when inevitable happened, and she told him of her pregnancy, the response was quick.

"You're fired," he would say, succinctly.

That was the end of the romance as far as he was concerned but crisis was created for the girl. What could she do? Hale him into court on a paternity charge and see her name all over the daily paper? Tell his wife? One girl did just that. She accomplished nothing. The wife had a home, family, pride and position to protect. She was not interested in what her husband did during his office hours. Besides, he had explained that she was fired for inefficiency, so this was an obvious attempt at blackmail.

Not all husbands have the inclination, time or money for extra-curricular affairs. Some seem to have surfeit of desire for their legal wives, coupled with a compulsion to inflict pain on them. It was a rare week that did not bring a woman to my office exhibiting evidence of her husband's brutality.

Polio victims came to my clinic in wheelchairs, their bodies so warped and twisted they were unable to lie on the table in normal position. I have operated on some of them with crippled feet resting on my shoulders, the only way it could be done. Nor were casts a novelty. There were patients wearing every known type of cast; some encased from neck to hip, so completely locked in plaster-of-Paris that one could not understand how their pregnancies had been accomplished. Many women told me they had to be aborted because they were wage earners for the family. The husband had been bedridden for months or years with a broken back, crushed pelvis or similar difficulty. One girl who came to me said she had only $15 for the operation. Her husband, she said, had a "bad back." And yet he had managed to make her pregnant. Some old goats could manage it with one foot in the grave and the other on a banana peel.

CHAPTER EIGHT

Portland, Oregon was a sprawling, lusty riverfront town, not yet quite a city in 1890 when Dr. Albert Littlefield established an office above a hardware store on Front Street. This middle-aged, unobtrusive physician was Oregon's first abortionist.

Dr. Littlefield's practice was to pass through many hands in the years after his death. It is worth noting that it operated, unharassed by law or busybodies for 65 years, never closing its door during that long time.

One of the men who brought distinction to the specialized practice began by Dr. Littlefield was Dr. Ed Stewart. I was first introduced to him by Dr. Watts who at one time was his associate. In truth, it was Watts who taught Stewart his successful surgery techniques.

I was impressed from the onset with Stewart, both as a man and doctor. He was then in his early fifties, straight as a ruler and apparently in superb physical condition. He had a keen mind and a constitution which carried him easily through the back-breaking hours of steady work in his surgery. He came from one of Oregon's pioneer families and for years remained a brilliant surgeon. Like Watts, he at first interspersed a general practice with occasional abortions for humanitarian reasons. Eventually, the abortion practice absorbed all of his time and he never seemed to regret it.

Dr. Stewart was an avid spokesman for loved hunting and fishing. He owned and operated a racing stable and played an important role in making horse racing a respected activity in Oregon. He was a cultured man, without pretensions. A connoisseur of art, he kept impressive collections of paintings both in his clinic and his home. He spent a great deal of money on worthy causes, including sizable grants he made on an anonymous basis to colleges and medical schools. Like the hero of Llyod C. Douglas's "Magnificent Obsession," he made these gifts under pledge of absolute secrecy. He was a very generous man.

This was my predecessor in the operations of the long established—and since 1951, notorious—Stewart Clinic, located in the Broadway Building along with mine.

Stewart, I met occasionally in the lobby or elevator. As the months passed, I noticed that his walk was less sprightly, his coloring not as healthy and his attitude not as confident as it had once been. The rumor was that he would soon dispose of his practice to a Seattle physician.

One morning, upon meeting in the elevator, he asked me to come to his office. "I've been wanting to talk to you," he said.

He came right to the point. "Ruth, would you like to buy this clinich?"

"Very much, I said. "But with what?"

He smiled and replied that that part of it was pretty well figured out. I listened carefully for half an hour. First, he explained his illness. For more than ten years he had suffered with a heart ailment, but in the past three years it had become seriously aggravated. A few days before, two of his fellow doctors had confronted him with a dire prognosis. If he wanted to continue living, he would have to retire and take it easy.

"You know," he said, "I've had this clinic for a good many years. It's been my life's work, and my only work. As I look back now, the years I spent in general practice, as a physician and surgeon, were only a preparation for the important work I've been doing since." He spoke slowly, candidly and thoughtfully.

"I know that many people look down on our profession. Some on religious grounds; others who are sincerely opposed to childbirth control on personal grounds; and others through ignorance who are mistakenly attempting to play the role of 'do-gooders,' trying to change nature to fit their particular prejudices."

I merely nodded, as he continued.

"All of these beliefs, sincere or crackpot, have bothered me very little. When it comes to weighing values, the appreciation of the hundreds of women I've helped—yes! And that of their husbands and lovers—paramount. Hasn't that been your attitude, too?"

I was listening so raptly that the abrupt question startled me. I said, "Yes, of course, it has."

He smiled and nodded. "I was sure of that. Now, let's get down to facts. I have to give up my clinic, something that I hate to do. I've built it up into what is considered the finest place of its kind in the United States and I'm proud of it."

"You have reason to be" I said.

"I've been considering just closing the doors, going out of business, rather than letting it fall into the hands of an unscrupulous practitioner. But this would impose hardships on many patients as well as friends in the medical profession who send their cased to me. No! I decided that going out of business is not the solution. I would like to turn over the practice to you."

As I gathered the drift of his talk, I was a little frightened. For the first time in my life, I wondered if I were equal to the challenge, taking over what was surely the most famous clinic of its kind in the Pacific Northwest if not anywhere. I tried to find words to articulate my doubts, but Dr. Stewart did not let me speak.

"This offer is not being made on the spur of the moment," he continued. "I've been giving it a lot of thought. Several doctors want to buy me out. One or two are among the most skilled abortionist in the country. They could pay more than you. But more than money is involved. I would like this clinic to continue to be the best. With you, I can be sure of that."

"For a good many years," he went on, "abortion operations have been largely a male doctor's profession. But that Is changing. Without prying, Ruth, I've learned a lot about you and your associates. And by observing and talking with my patients, I've learned an old truth. In times of stress, a woman turns to a woman."

So, it was done. The price was a solid round figure, a lot of money but a bargain for a really excellent practice. The terms for paying it were generous. Dr. Stewart's rooms were beautifully furnished. There were eleven of them and they took up nearly the whole eighth floor of the Broadway Building. His reputation had been flawless and his name was known throughout the Northwest wherever women were in trouble. I kept the name "Stewart Clinic" on my doors.

My new clinic flourished. It was 1945 when I took it over and, once again, a catastrophic world war had brought a tremendous rush of work for those in my profession. In the next six years, before my world fell apart, I was to earn a great deal of money. Patients came to me not only from all over Oregon, but from throughout California, Nevada, Washington, Idaho and even further points. I added another doctor to my staff, two nurses and an office manager. These were my busiest, and in many ways, happiest, years.

Always a gregarious woman, I found time to work hard and also for fun. I began seeking my friendships among those who lived and worked at night—club owners, musicians, entertainers, other nocturnal people. They were good company and we got along famously, perhaps because such people were not so hide-bound and prudish and were as quick to accept me as I was to accept them.

Those happy, prosperous years in the Stewart Clinic were to be cut short by a series of events which I had never anticipated. While the thought of arrest might have crossed my mind at times, I never thought of myself as the central figure in a case celebre.

There was nothing secret about the operations of the Stewart Clinic in the Broadway Building. We had no locks on any of the doors except the one leading to a hall, which we locked at night. The majority of our cases were referrals from licenses physicians and surgeons. A great many cases even came to me from a prominent Catholic gynecologist who would tell women who insisted on an abortion to "go to the Broadway Building and ask for Dr. Ruth."

CHAPTER NINE

In the movies, they always depict the fallen woman sneaking up a dirty, rickety stairway to a dismal room—or making her way, furtively, into a dark alley that leads to a decrepit shack where some alcoholic doctor or untutored butcher performs the abortion.

A clinic such as mine was not that way at all. It was a bright, cheerful place where women's problems were handled quickly, efficiently and with dignity, no matter what the circumstances of the patient.

I do not honestly know how many abortions I have performed in the half century I have made this work my profession. Certainly, they run into the thousands. It has been suggested that I have done as many as 40,000 such operations since 1918. The figure sounds high, but it is quite possible.

And there is one figure of which I am entirely certain. In all those abortions over all those years, I never lost a single patient.

I have heard a number of physicians say that no one can perform as many abortions as I have done without losing a patient. They talk about the dangers of rupturing or perforating a womb and the ever-present danger of hemorrhage.

These doctors, whose knowledge of abortion techniques is miniscule at best, are talking through their hats. I have a light touch and I have never perforated a uterus.

I can recall, over the years, eight or nine, perhaps ten cases, in which there was a serious bleeding. Each of these cases I sent to a hospital, primarily for the patient's peace of mind. I could have dealt with the hemorrhage, but thought it best, all things considered, for the woman to have hospital treatment.

Patients who came to my clinics were sometimes violently ill when they arrived. I've had husbands bring their wives to me so sick they had to be carried into my office.

Sometimes, a woman with a different pregnancy suffers from pernicious vomiting. They are so ridden with nausea they cannot even hold water on their stomachs. Their family doctors would give them an injection or two—and then refer them to me.

The rapid recovery which comes from abortion to a woman suffering in such a way is nothing short of amazing. I remember cases where the woman was too ill to stand. Ten minutes after the operation these women were sipping tea and eating crackers in my clinic's little kitchenette.

The Pullman kitchen in my office lounge was completely equipped and one of my nurses was a wonderful cook. Our luncheons were so tasty we sometimes had as many as eight or ten guests. Not only patients, but business friends as well. Those were times with lots of laughs and good-natured kidding. I accused my nurse of putting out a sign on the street: "Try Barnett's Blue Plate Special."

We dealt with the comic and the tragi-comic. There were elements of amusement in the arrival, one day during World War II, of four uniformed Soviet women officers from a Russian ship berthed at Swan Island for repairs. One was a captain. The four Russian women were accompanied by a Soviet male official who acted as an interpreter to explain their problem — they were pregnant. Apparently, free love, Communist style, was practiced on the Soviet Union's ships.

One day a lovely, middle-aged woman came to see me. She told her son had gone to Korea and, before leaving, made her promise to look after his wife's expected baby so his wife could get back to work in a defense plant. Now, there was an unexpected turn which had upset all these-laid plans. Grandmother was pregnant.

During World War II, a woman welder from the Kaiser shipyards came to me. I thought her costume rather quaint. She wore a tin safety hat, a welder's work-stained overalls, ship-yard boots— and a full-length mink coat.

There were those cases which bordered on fatal tragedy. I re-call a woman who came to me with her husband after her family doctor has said there was nothing seriously wrong with her and he could not approve an abortion. I took a blood sample from the woman and sent it to a lab for analysis. The woman was seriously ill with kidney disease and, in my opinion, childbirth would have killed her. She got her abortion.

Another woman came to me on instructions from her family physician. This doctor and an associate had diagnosed her to be suffering tuberculosis of the bone. Both recommended ter-mination of her pregnancy. These two physicians had made a wise decision. But I could not help but wonder what would have happened to this woman if, because of religious convictions, the doctors had not recommended she have an abortion. Such a decision, it is clear to me, should be made by a husband and wife after they are given a frank appraisal of the woman's physical condition by a competent doctor.

Unwanted pregnancy is no respecter of persons. Among my patients have been those of fabled wealth and high position. And there have been others who were dirty poor.

A widow came to me who was so desperately poor she was rearing her family of five children by cutting firewood. The man responsible for her sixth pregnancy was married. His Catholic wife refused to consent to a divorce.

Faced with the prospect of six mouths to feed, six bodies to clothe and very little money, she had tried all the home remed-ies in an effort to miscarry only to become sick and feverish. Be-fore she left the clinic, my nurse took her home address. We sent a big box of clothing for the children and a dress and warm coat for the woodcutter. But my greatest satisfaction was my belief that I had saved her from possible death from infection.

Some years ago, my husband, Earl Bush, and I had a house guest at our Eastern Oregon ranch. She was a stunning, prema-turely gray woman with whom we were laughingly reminiscing when she turned to me and said:

"Do you remember, Ruth, the time I came to you and you took care of me?"

I said I did, and she recalled that she had been secretary to the governor of Oregon when she had missed a couple of periods. She had mentioned it to an intimate friend, a physician who didn't bother to examine her, merely pooh-poohed the idea that she could be pregnant. "An early change of life," he had called it.

"You know, Ruth," she said. "When the morning sickness hit me, I nearly jumped out of my hotel room window. But then I thought of you.

"The next day I was back at my desk in Salem and up to my eyebrows in a tough political campaign. Nobody was any the wise—not even the governor."

Several years before the Portland crack-down on abortions, San Francisco went through similar turmoil. Many San Francisco women then came to me.

Pauline was a stunning Bay Area woman who told me of her experience in the City By The Golden Gate—a city where consumption of alcoholic beverages and promiscuity is as high as anywhere in the land.

Pregnant and unable to find a competent abortionist, Pauline met a bartender who told her he could put her in touch with a doctor for $100. He neglected to tell her this "doctor" was a barber. She paid the $100 and the bartender sent her to meet the "doctor" in a tumble-down building in the San Francisco slums. Once there, she was told she would have to be blindfolded and taken to a trailer camp on the outskirts of the city. She senses that the entire set-up was phony and told the abortion ring she was no longer interested.

Desperate, she telephoned one of San Francisco's leading obstetricians. This doctor had his nurse telephone me long-distance and make an appointment.

Pauline caught the first available airplane and when she walked into my office she was amazed by its cleanliness and the tasteful furnishings. Most of all she was surprised by the way we conducted business. We had no secrecy in those days.

Women who came and went at my clinic with scarcely any more fuss than there would be in keeping an appointment at a beauty salon. Many girls came to me during their lunch hour and returned to work the same afternoon with no distress.

Of all my thousands of cases, there is one that stands out for its depth of poignancy. In one respect, the case was unique. It was brought to me by "Baron."

Baron, you must understand, was a Seeing-Eye dog. His mistress had been given my name by a mutual friend. Desperately in love with her man, she had become pregnant. To her, in her darkness, marriage was unthinkable. When the beautiful big dog let her into my office, my receptionist, to put it mildly, was a bit surprised.

Baron was visibly nervous. His mistress reassured him with a gentle voice, told him to lie down and wait for her in the consultation room while the nurse led her into surgery. It was a new and strange experience for Baron to be left by his mistress in strange surroundings. He lay there, alert to every sound and movement while I operated. When she returned, he seemed to sense her feeling of relief. He romped and jumped like a puppy. And before they left the office, Baron nuzzled each of us in turn. It was as though the god, through some instinct, was expressing gratitude.

That's the one case I shall never forget.

CHAPTER TEN

The great loves of my life have been my work, my grandchildren, fishing and racehorses.

During the years I was married to Earl Bush, we had a fine string of thoroughbreds.

Earl had been a member of the famed Canadian Mounties as a young man and all his life he had loved horses. During my childhood in Hood River, Dad had always been a horse trader and as far back as I can remember, he was bringing home strange horses and putting either my sister or me atop them. I, too, had developed a love of horses and when Earl and I first met it was this mutual interest which nurtured our love.

A short time after we met, we bought a brood mare in foal. Her registered name was "Irene F" and the filly colt she presented us had hard going at the start. She broke out with boils and, despite the best veterinary care, seemed destined for an early grave.

When the time came to register the ailing colt with the Jockey Club, there was a lot of argument about the name. Earl had the final say and he seemed to sum things up when he said, "Oh, let's call her 'Irene's Angel.' That's what she'll be before long. She's a mighty sick little filly."

Happily, my husband's prediction was wrong. Irene's Angel grew into a beautiful mare and was the pet of horsemen wherever she went.

When she was two years old, she romped home winner of the Best Oregon Bred Horse Futurity at the Oregon State Fair. After that, she won with a regularity that delighted racegoers. Devotees of the sport came to know she would regularly either be a winner or up front in the money.

We had better than average luck with nearly all our horses, winning many races. And the thrill of winning a race with your own horse never seems to diminish. There is no thrill in the world like watching a horse you have reared and helped train coming down the stretch to capture the honors.

Another horse of ours, Embaco, duplicated Irene's Angel's feat of winning the Best Oregon Bred Horse Futurity as a two-year-old and, a year later, led the field in the derby for the best Oregon bred three-year-olds.

In both of these races, the track was a sea of mud. But that meant nothing to Embaco. He got out in front at the gate and stayed there. He wasn't a horse to have any mud flung in his face.

I mention Embaco's prowess as a "mudder," because when my troubles came in 1951 a friend hinted to me it might be best to take my name off Oregon race programs. The word was out that the racing board did not care for such "racy" publicity as I had been receiving.

I could never see the logic in this. Would disclaiming ownership of a thoroughbred make that publicity any less obnoxious? Would my racehorses have been less crowd pleasing? Would they sulk and fail to run their best, because I was on trial? Should my horses have been put out to pasture because I was an accused abortionist?

When I walk through the crowds at Portland Meadows, even today, nodding and smiling at friends, I can see many patients of mine. These are people who once came to me in distress. These are people whom I not only aided but shielded from publicity and shame. Among them are some of the track's best patrons. Some of them are owners of horses waiting in the barns across the track.

I'm sure that Irene's Angle, Mags, Big Boy, Embaco, Chicago Cotton, Pharlita, Red Top and Easter Kay never cared a whit about my profession.

The original promoters of Portland Meadows knew my profession when they accepted my money. They knew the nature of

Dr. Edgar Stewart's practice when they accepted his money.

When the Columbia River flooded the track in 1948, my abortion money was good enough to help clean up the mud from the paddock, the grandstand and even the swank clubhouse where the august racing board gathered.

When the track suffered financial reverses and went on the rocks, my abortion dollars were good enough to help reopen it. I don't regret any of the money I spent in furthering the "sport of kings" in Oregon. Just seeing that headline favored by sports' writers, "Irene's Angle Used Her Wings Again Today" made it all worthwhile.

I loved horse racing with a mad passion.

And I hate hypocrisy.

CHAPTER ELEVEN

One of the arguments for legalizing abortion is so compelling, has such a great emotional appeal, that the most stubborn diehards quail before it.

Early in 1967, the Senate Judiciary Committee of the Oregon Legislature (one of about 25 state legislatures in the U.S. considering liberalization of the abortion laws) held public hearings on proposals to legalize abortion in a number of cases.

A prominent Catholic gynecologist who opposed the new legislation was cornered after the hearings by two women who favored the bill. "What would you do, Doctor," asked one of them, "if a young girl was brought to you, pregnant, the victim of forcible rape?"

His answer was glib enough. "Oh, in rape cases we can give drugs to prevent conception," he said. When I was told of this dialogue, it seemed to me he was making an argument for, and not, against the abortion. But uppermost in my mind was my vivid recollection of Doreen.

Just after World War II, while I was still operating openly in the Stewart Clinic, my receptionist had a telephone call from Doreen's aunt. Doreen, the aunt said, had been sexually assaulted by three teen-age boys in a vacant house in the Albina district. Afraid to tell her parents about what had happened to her, she had gone to her aunt, bleeding and hysterical.

The aunt, in turn, had taken the girl to her mother and required her to tell her mother of her experience. In time, she had shown signs of pregnancy. The father, a railway employee, had been advised. Because the family had no regular doctor, the girl was taken to first one doctor, then to a second, finally to a third.

Each had refused to terminate the pregnancy.

My receptionist heard this poignant story with growing compassion. But the staggering, almost incredible punch line had yet to come.

Doreen was only eleven years old.

Frankly, when I was told about the case, I did not want it. I was afraid, for one thing, that the girl's cervix would be terribly constricted. It seemed to me, despite the aunt's assertion that "she's well developed for her age, more like a girl of 13 or 14," that here was a case for the gynecologists.

The family, however, was adamant in its insistence that I was the only one who could help Doreen. As usual, I found it hard to turn them away. Reluctantly, I agreed to give the girl an examination, not promising anything further.

Mother, father and aunt all came with Doreen to the clinic. She was, superficially, well-developed for her age. But it was equally obvious that she was still very much a child. She knew nothing of sex, knew only that "something" had happened to her. Badly frightened as the mere thought of a physical examination, she was in mild hysteria. I gave her a grain and a half of Nembutal to calm her, but she was frantic on the examination table. Her organs, as I suspected, were yet undeveloped. But I thought I could help her.

"You will have to calm her down," I told the mother. "When you come back again, she must be more composed."

Surprisingly, Doreen turned out to be a good patient. While I operated, I talked to her in a soothing voice and she seemed to draw some inner strength from the knowledge that I was helping her. I told her she must try to forget her experience and should never tell anyone in the future about it. The operation went a lot easier that I had thought it would and there were no complications.

When it was all over, my receptionist asked Doreen's aunt how she had happened to bring the girl to me. Who had told her about my clinic? The aunt smiled. "Dr. Ruth has forgotten me, of course," she said. "But I was one of her patients years ago."

It is my personal belief that the only requirement for an abortion, under any circumstances, should be the desire of the woman—whatever her reason—to interrupt her pregnancy.

While this is my view, I have listened with patience to the convictions of others on the subject. And yet I cannot understand any religious or ethical code which would deny an abortion to a young girl in Doreen's tragic circumstances.

An entirely different case which came to us at the Stewart Clinic was that of the woman my staff called the "walking skeleton."

The "walking skeleton" was the mother of nine children. She was nearly six feet tall, but when she came to me and I had her step on the scales in my office she weighed only 102 pounds.

Her skin hung in folds. She had suffered dreadfully with pernicious vomiting. When she told her family doctor, she was fearful of another confinement, he told her, "You've had nine children. I see no real reason you can't have another one." I cannot understand his lack of concern over the fact that in 10 weeks of pregnancy she had lost 38 pounds. In my experience, most expectant mothers tend to gain rather than lose weight.

The "skeleton" was one of those cases which respond almost immediately to surgery. We kept her at the clinic for three hours or so after the operation. She was suddenly ravenous. In the kitchenette I fixed her some crackers and bouillon. She ate as though famished, which the poor woman was, and left the clinic in almost buoyant spirits.

A clinic such as the Stewart Clinic was, in spite of the daily quota of problems, a sort of "Peyton Place" in miniature. Our principal concern, of course was the women who came to us, each of them in what some humorist has described as an "interesting condition." But tangential to this abiding, grimly serious business were little sub-plots from the human comedy—some as forbidding as the two stories I have just related, others genuinely amusing.

In 1949, we had our greatest mystery. Dorothy, my receptionist, came to the building one morning to open the office, as usual, at 9 a.m. She found the front door, which opened on the waiting room, unlocked. There was also the usual practice.

She noticed the pillows on the davenport were disarranged and went to straighten them. To her surprise, on the davenport was a tiny baby girl, wrapped in a torn blanket, obviously not more than twenty-four hours old.

Dorothy noticed the baby had a bluish tinge, so she rushed it to the surgery and held it over the sterilizer to warm it. She wrapped the baby in sheets, towels, and absorbent cotton until she was in a snug cocoon. Then she telephoned Bea, my office nurse, and told her to hurry down to the clinic. Next, she telephoned my daughter, Margaret, who had a baby of her own. She asked Margaret to bring diapers, condensed milk and other baby paraphernalia to the office. After Bea had checked the baby over, Margaret took her home to care for her.

When I came down to the office, I told the girls we would have to notify the authorities. I telephoned the Women's Protective Division of the police department and made the necessary arrangements for institutional care. Helen, another of my nurses, took an immediate liking to the baby. She was in her late 30's at the time, had never been able to have children of her own. She wanted the baby desperately and I was able, with friends in high places, to arrange for a speedy legal adoption. Today, the foundling left in my waiting room is a beautiful young lady, red-haired and green-eyed, a fine student. Her adoptive parents have told her how she came to be theirs.

How did the baby get into my waiting room? Who left her? We have never learned the answer. The Broadway Building's street entrance was unlocked at 8 a.m. each morning and there was nearly an hour in which someone could have left her there. Ellen recalled a red-harried woman who was "too far along" for us to help who may have left her unwanted baby there. But we could never be sure to she was the one. There were so many who came to us too late to be helped and we could only advise them to have their babies, put them up for adoption. One of them must have decided to hand us her "problem" in more direct fashion.

And, shades of "Peyton Place," there was time a highly-sophisticated girl with auburn hair and expensive clothes was sent to us by her boyfriend, a high-ranking Portland police officer. Dorothy, the receptionist, had trouble getting answers to her questions about her last menstruation. Finally, unable to hedge any longer, the gal made a bold proposition.

"I'm not really pregnant," she said, "but he thinks I am. He gave me this $300 and I want you to take $100 and tell him you took care of me."

Dorothy, who was a friend of the police officer, was quick-witted. She told the girl she wanted to examine the money—to make sure it was not marked. When the girl handed Dorothy the money, Dorothy quickly opened the safe and locked the money inside. "I'll have to do some checking to make sure the whole arrangement is all right with Dr. Ruth," she said. "You come back tomorrow, and we'll see about your $200."

After the woman left, Dorothy telephoned the police officer, asked him to meet her for a cup of coffee. When they met, she handed him his $300, told him his mistress was not pregnant. He was a surprised, and suddenly wiser, gendarme.

The girlfriend never came back to the clinic.

CHAPTER TWELVE

My world fell apart on the afternoon of July 6, 1951. I was in eastern Oregon, spending a long holiday weekend with my husband and several guests at our ranch. Four of us were on the range, hunting strays in the canyons and draws of the sagebrush country when the bad news came by telephone—replayed from Portland to Burns and the cookhouse of the Bush Ranch in the high desert. The cook was waiting when we rode in.

"Portland wants you," she said. It's urgent."

Two thoughts came instantly to mind: Margaret, just recovering from a polio attack, had suffered a relapse, or something had gone wrong at the clinic—always a possibility in spite of precautions taken. Whatever it was, I did not wish to discuss it on the cookhouse phone, a crank-equipped, wall instrument, hooked to a twenty-party line.

The call was transferred to a phone booth at Riley, a hamlet three miles distant containing service station, general store, garage and a few weather-beaten houses.

"Ready with Portland," the operator said.

"Margaret," I asked, "are you all right?"

"I'm fine," said my daughter, "but you're in trouble."

The clinic had been raided—the last thing I expected. True, there had been rumors, rumblings and whispers for weeks. But before leaving for the holiday, I learned from what the newspapers term an "authoritative source" that no legal action was contemplated against me. This, in effect, was a reaffirmation of the unwritten agreement under which I had always run m clinics: No persecution unless there was a death.

"There's a warrant out for your arrest," Margaret said.

A raiding party of sixteen including the sheriff, city police officers, a special investigator for the D.A., a lawyer on the D.A.'s staff, newspaper reporter and photographer had stormed into the office.

"A big, Hollywood-type production," she said. "Brave lads in blue stomping up and down, flash-bulbs poppin'. They even had a hospital alerted, and an ambulance standing by, in case they found a patient on the table."

The receptionist, nurse and doctor who worked for me had been arrested and taken to the Multnomah County courthouse. They were still there, as far as Margaret knew, being held incommunicado.

"That's only the beginning," she continued. "They've been out to our house and are looking for you everywhere. They've been talking about you on the police radio, looking for your car. They've got roadblocks out."

The rest was cloak-and-dagger stuff. Margaret promised to get in touch with my attorneys and see if arrangements could be made for bail. And she would try to learn what had happened to my associates who had been arrested.

I returned to the Bush Ranch where Earl and our guests waited on the patio. I told them what had happened. They were as stunned as I, blankly silent for a moment, then all began talking at once.

"I've got to get back to Portland," I said. "Please, Earl, we're going the long way. I don't care how much extra driving it means—five hundred, even a thousand miles. I'm going to walk into the courthouse and give myself up. They'd like to catch me at a roadblock, with a lot of fanfare and pictures and newspaper headlines saying I was arrested while trying to get away. I'm not going to be trapped like that. I've never run away from anything, and I won't start now.

"All right," he said. "The long way it is."

We were three or four minutes from the ranch gate, heading east for a false start, when a police car passed. As we climbed the hill east of Riley, we looked back. It was turning into the ranch. I missed the arrest by only a few minutes.

As we drove along, I began to realize how little I knew of the Oregon laws pertaining abortion. They had never really interested me until that terrible day. The state statute, written in 1864, about the same time legislation had also been enacted making it illegal for a person to become a doctor merely by hanging out a shingle, had remained virtually unchanged. That much I knew. But I had never concerned with the exact wording of that statute. For that matter, neither had the doctors who referred their desperate patients to me, nor any of the previous district attorneys of Oregon.

There is not as strange as it is may sound. My clinic had been in existence for more than sixty-five years in various locations, under various ownerships. In all that time there was no attempt to halt its operations. This was not because hush money had been spread around. Neither I nor predecessors had ever paid or been asked to pay for the privilege of operating.

Portland was, perhaps, unique in this respect. The duly elected officers of the law, members of the medical profession and state medical board knew we were in business. Trying to conceal the clinic, or its purpose, would have been as impossible as hiding an elephant in the parlor. Thousands of women had passed through our doors, of all colors, races and creeds and from various walks of life. The archaic statue had never been considered.

Why not, I wondered, had we been raided? Earl and I rode in silence most of the time, speaking suddenly only to punctuate a private, troubled thought, such as his wry comment: "Maybe blackmail's a good investment."

I had been worrying about certain patients. We recalled a woman who had contacted us several months before. She was a former resident of Earl's hometown, an acquaintance. After her vague and half-threatening phone call, we met her. She announced that my office would be raided, but the raid could be prevented if I gave her $10,000 in cash.

I did not believe her and told her so.

She took a black notebook from her purse. She said she was the emissary for a group consisting of an investigator on the D.A's staff, a city police detective, an inspector for the state medical board and a newspaper reporter. She had been selected to make the negotiations, she said, because she knew Earl well enough to speak bluntly.

"And how much of the $10,000 do you get?" I asked.

"Two thousand."

"Exactly what does the $10,000 buy?"

"Evidence," she said. "Do business with us, and every scrap of evidence—will be called off, and you'll have plenty of advance warning in the future."

"You're making all this up," I said.

"I can prove I'm not."

She opened the notebook and read entries which listed, by dates, the number of patients who had come to my office the previous week. Then she named, and described, two women had posed as prospective patients but were working for the special investigator employed by the district attorney.

"Ten thousand is a lot of money," I said.

She smiled. "They said you could dig it up somehow."

"No!" I told her. "I won't."

And I did not. The deadline she set—midnight of the day before the raid—come and went. When I checked with the office staff, I found that her list of patients was correct. Then, I wondered if her prediction would also turn out to be accurate. I inquired, through my own sources, if the clinic should be closed rather than allow it to be raided. Back came the same authoritative reply: Nothing had changed. I accepted their word, forgot whatever fears I had and left for the ranch.

Now, I was sorry not to have questioned the woman with the black notebook more closely. What, I wondered, was the evidence, against me?

About 1 a.m. we reached Pendleton, the Round-Up city, where we stopped long enough to buy the late-edition Portland newspaper. Then we continued homeward. I turned on the map light and saw my name in big black headlines for the first time in my life.

"How bad it is?" Earl asked me.

It was a few moments before I could answer him. "Worse than I ever imagined," I said.

Here was my life's work vilified and smeared. I had long believed that every woman has the right of abortion if she believes it necessary. How could I believe otherwise after talking to thousands of women—sick, lame, frightened, and hungry—in need of help. I had worked hard to make my establishment a beautiful and friendly place, where every possible safeguard was taken against infection and accident. And where—most important of all—none need fear that today's secret would become tomorrow's idle gossip.

I was proud of the clinic and justly so.

And now the newspapers made it appear something between a plush-lined house of ill-fame and an abattoir catering specially to the young. "Several young women, one of high school age, were in the waiting room. One, apparently fearing arrest, ran screaming down the stairs," a newspaper reported. The dressing rooms and surgery were described as though the reporter had viewed them in some kind of private hallucination. Out of his welter of words emerged an image of dumb cattle waiting to be slaughtered by a sadistic butcher. All my years of work for hapless women had been drowned in a torrent of newspaper sensationalism.

We were a few blocks from the Columbia River ferry that would take us into the state of Washington when Earl stopped in front of a small all-night café. The parking lot was quiet and dark. Through the lighted window I could see the clock on the wall. It was 3 a.m. We went in, sat down at one end of the horse-shoe counter. We were the only customers, but not for long.

Headlights flashed through the windows as a state police car drove up and parked beside ours. Two officers emerged. One went to the rear of Earl's car, took a slip of paper from his pocket and beamed his flashlight on the license plate, as I watched through the window. It seemed an eternity before he shook his head. They were looking for my license number, not Earl's.

The officers came into the café and sat down at the other end of the counter, opposite us. They looked us over casually. Earl finished his coffee, paid the check and we walked out as slowly and nonchalantly as we could.

In a few minutes we were on the ferry, heading for the Washington shore. By 6 a.m. we reached the Evergreen Hotel in Vancouver, Washington. Fourteen hours of high-speed driving were exhausting. Earl took a hot bath and went to sleep. I lay awake, restless and fearful of what the next day would bring.

Vancouver, Washington lies just across the Columbia River from Portland. After a few hours rest we drove across the Interstate Bridge and directly to the Multnomah County Jail, stopping only once to telephone my attorney.

While an officer at the courthouse took my name and address, the room began filling up with people. Although Saturday is usually a quiet day, word of my arrival to turn myself in got around quickly. Reporters and photographers appeared as out of nowhere and were soon buzzing around us.

A uniformed officer stopped by the desk and said, apologetically, "Dr. Barnett, I'd rather have been anywhere else in the world than in your office yesterday." Then, the flashbulbs started popping and the reporters began their questions. My attorney, said, "No comment."

I was taken to the photographer to be "mugged." I remember being grateful that they did not hang a number around my neck. Another officer rolled my fingers on an ink pad and then put my fingerprints on a white card. Recently, more than 15 years later, he performed the same act. On the later occasion, he looked up at me with a concerned expression, "Say, Ruth," he said. "You're getting arthritis in your fingers." The way he said it told me he realized we had both grown a lot older.

My next stop was a crowded office, apparently used by the District Attorney and his staff. The newspapermen were there ahead of us, cameras and pencils poised. The District Attorney entered the room. He nodded perfunctorily. A special investigator and a deputy district attorney were to be the interrogators.

"We've been looking everywhere for you," the deputy D.A. said.

"I was at the ranch," I replied.

"We knew that, but we couldn't catch up with you."

He did not know how close they came, several times.

"I wanted to do it this way—give myself up," I said. "It took some doing, but we managed it."

"How?" a reporter asked.

I answered, "No comment."

Flashbulbs kept exploding. Cameras recorded the scene for the hungry front pages. I smiled. When I am angry, or hurt, I smile.

"This is no laughing matter" the deputy D.A. snapped. "It is a very serious charge, Dr. Barnett."

"I know," I said. I tried to control the defensive smile, but it kept coming back. I would have felt quite lost without a mask of some kind in that hostile room.

I spent an hour and a half being shunted from one room to another. As I was leaving, the smile relaxed into a weary sigh. Bail was arranged. We went from the courthouse to the clinic, where my receptionist, nurse and doctor awaited us. They had been trying to straighten things up, but the place looked as if a herd of elephants and stomped through it.

The staff gave me a step-by-step account, from the moment the police had swarmed into the building and told the elevator operator to touch nothing but the control lever. Several days later she was still wondering what else there might have been to touch. We had no secret alarm bells or electric buzzers. Why should we have had any alarm system when we had operated for so many years free of any trouble with the law?

The raiding procedure must have been adapted from a "B" grade movie. Sixteen people had charged in to arrest the three of them. They were loud and abusive. Women in the waiting room, guilty of no offense, were treated harshly. Those in the dressing rooms were terrified. One newspaper reported a woman behind a curtain, in an adjoining room, struggling desperately to get dressed.

The raiders ransacked the offices without a proper search warrant, yanked drawers out of desks and cabinets and spilled their contents on the floor. They confiscated unopened mail, a file of paid bills and current bills. They took several hundred dollars in cash—never returned to this day—that was kept on hand for operating expenses and salaries. One deputy, who must have been a fan of Sax Rohmer's Fu Manchu stories, was certain that the hand-carved Chinese desk contained secret drawers and panels. When he couldn't find them, he threatened to smash the desk, but desisted when the receptionist protested vigorously.

Looking back, I believe they were looking for a filing system they could bundle it up and cart away: a list of patients together with the names of doctors who had sent them to us. But identities of those who came to us for help were well hiding. There was no such file.

They scooped up every instrument they could find, no matter what the design or purpose. And, it was in this connection that their thirst for melodrama was finally satisfied. There was an ornamental grille installed beneath a window, to hide an unsightly heating arrangement. It was equipped with knobs or handles that were clearly visible and easily grasped. Behind the grille, a detective found several packages of instruments. Flashbulbs popped again. Here was a secret cache!

Those instruments were the onetime property of the late Dr. Stewart, former owner of the clinic who had left them behind when I bought the practice. He had discarded them for new and better instruments. They were almost antiques, a type used at the turn of the century. They might have been of interest as rusty museum pieces, but certainly had no value of modern surgery. We stored them back of the "secret" panel to get them out of the way. Surgical instruments are not disposable as paper towels. There is always possibility they will be removed from a trash can or be purchased from a second-hand store and then be used by an untrained, unskilled person. Behind the grille had seemed to us the best place for them.

After the raid, the staff was held in the courthouse for hours and questioned at length before being allowed to use a telephone. Bail had been arranged in the closing minutes of the business day.

"We'll fight this," I told them. "We'll have the best legal advice I can get."

Before there could be an indictment, there had to be evidence. In all my years of practice, no one had ever gone—or had cause to go—to the law enforcement people with a complaint. Now, it seemed, there was evidence to present to a grand jury. Somebody had talked. But who and about what?

Before long, of course, we found out. The state's case was built around a girl of seventeen who had been treated, months before by my staff while I was away on vacation. I'll call her Ann Kelly. That is not her name, but I shall not add to the public exposure she and her family suffered on the witness stand. Ann was slender and pretty, considerably underweight when she first came to us. Her hair, normally, was a lustrous brown; her eyes a deep blue.

Ann lived with her mother and father in a small house in a small town—its identity not important. Her parents were honest, decent people, hardworking and God-fearing. They had reared two sons and had seen them married and settled in homes of their own. Ann was their youngest child.

Mrs. Kelly had told her daughter, vaguely and fumblingly, to be careful when she went out with boys. But she had neglected to tell her not to be alone in a family home with an older first cousin. On a bright September day, she opened the door to welcome him and was raped, quickly, brutally. The cousin? Shortly thereafter he left Oregon for a distant and more salubrious climate.

Ann had not known much about sex. But she learned soon enough. The moon waxed and waned. Nausea overcame her. She began losing her breakfast. Like many others she searched the shelves of a serve-yourself drugstore for a nostrum and found a patent medicine which, the label said, would ease the pains of her menses and combat "irregularity." She dosed herself heavily, but only felt worse.

A second month went by. Ann had always been a cheerful child. Now she turned glum. She could not eat and lost weight alarmingly. She was given to long silences, staring at the wall into the dreaded future, wondering what her parents and friends would say, how the people of her town would react when she could no longer hide her pregnancy.

And there were vaginal discharges now—infection. This may have been due to the lack of proper care at the time of the sexual attack. Or it may have had its cause elsewhere. The source and extent of this infection were to become the subject of bitter debate at my trial. Whatever the cause, the noxious discharge aggravated Ann's distress.

At Christmas time, Ann finally was forced to tell her mother what had happened. Despair suffused the household. Ann was sent, alone, to the office of a woman physician. She was examined—the manner and thoroughness of the examination also to be subjects of harsh courtroom debate—and her pregnancy was confirmed. She was advised to have the pregnancy continue and was told that arrangements could, and would, be made for her medical and hospital care.

There was a tearful family conference. The Kellys were afraid that a child, born of such a union, would be less than normal. The Kellys agreed Ann should not be forced to bear her cousin's child.

Ann's mother took her to another physician, a man of unimpeachable reputation in the community. When he heard that the pregnancy had resulted from a rape by a cousin, he gave Ann my address. This was later admitted by the prosecution in court, though the doctor's name was withheld at our request.

Ann and her mother appeared at my clinic. Mrs. Kelly told the receptionist the story, and how desperately she hoped for help.

That help was forthcoming the next day. After a short recuperation, Ann went home, no longer glum and silent. She faced her friends and neighbors without fear of discovery and continued the normal pattern of her life.

The Kellys were grateful to us, Ann most of all. But the cost of the operation had bitten deeply into their small savings. It seemed only reasonable to them, therefore, that the cousin responsible should pay at least a part. They wrote to him. But when their letters brought no reply, they decided on another tack. Safe in another state, he might ignore their pleas, but they thought he would listen to the law. The Kellys went to see the district attorney of their downstate county, explaining they sought no publicity, did not want the cousin jailed but just frightened enough to pay his share. Would he write a letter using big, official words? Would he throw a scare into the rapist? Enough of a scare so the offender would rush to the post office with a money order to cover the expenses of Ann's operation?

The reaction to the Kellys request was not exactly what they had anticipated. Indeed, the D.A. was not speaking of rape, brutal and criminal though it had been. That apparently did not concern him, nor the fate of the victim. No prosecution was planned against the cousin, either then or later. But the operation—abortion was against the law. He told the Kellys they would be compounding a felony if they refused to divulge the details.

So the machinery which brought my arrest was set in motion. Confused, frightened by threats of arrest and prison, the Kellys talked freely. Statements were taken and signed. These went to the Oregon State Medical Board and then to the office of the district attorney for Multnomah County. The old by tacit understanding—no death, no prosecution—was pushed aside by heavy newspaper and political pressures. Though deeply disturbed and unwilling to hurt those who had helped them, the Kellys were forced to testify before a grand jury and a secret indictment was returned. Then the raiders swooped down on my clinic.

The State of Oregon's case was to be built around frail Ann Kelly, the girl we had succored and who had been given a new chance to lead a normal, healthy life. Pregnancy that was not her fault had been a secret within her family. Now, it was to be revealed on the witness stand and in the newspapers. Ann and her parents were to learn how cruel small-town mores can be, while her cousin was never to be exposed, permitted to go his merry way.

CHAPTER THIRTEEN

When the first shock of arrest had spent itself and I was able to think clearly, I realized the need of legal advice. My knowledge of attorneys was limited, however. An attorney, up to then, had been someone who prepared a lease or bill of sale. I had never been in trouble with the law before and I was 58 years old.

With the help of friends, I selected a young lawyer who was highly regarded and had a pleasing courtroom appearance. Unfortunately, he had no experience with a case like mine. The dreary tragedies of pregnant women were only something he had read about in books. He knew nothing of the horrors faced by a daughter in distress, a mother smothered in routine household chores, a woman raped.

I believe he condemned Ann—the girl the state had forced to testify against me—as a fallen woman past redemption who should be exposed.

Once engaged, my lawyer's first instructions were to keep the office doors locked and break off associates with all prospective patients as well as with the physicians who sent me patients. I was shocked. How could he sit there and tell me I must severe all my connections, all the social and professional relationships I had spent a lifetime building? How could he expect me to terminate, abruptly, my life's work?

I knew that what he demanded was impossible. Even if I were to set sail for Timbuctoo, some patients, or their friends, would seek me out, somehow. Wherever I went, they would come to weep of my doorstep. And I knew I could not turn them away.

Nevertheless, I tried to follow his advice. In those last six months of 1951, there were beseeching phone calls, pleading letters and weeping mothers knocking at the door. My answer was, "I'm sorry, but I can't help you. The office is closed. I'm under indictment." And I, in turn, would entreat them not to call me again, telling them my attorney had forbidden me to work.

December came with all the attendant Yuletide rush and it began to look as though I would be able to finish out that disastrous year with some peace of mind. But two weeks before Christmas there came another appeal. A young woman came to my home, told me she was divorced but had custody of three small children. Her mother lived with her and took care of the children while she worked to support them. But now she was pregnant. The man responsible was in Korea, thousands of miles away. She needed help desperately.

I told the young woman it was impossible for me to help her, but I had heard there was a doctor in a certain Seattle office building who might be able to do something for her. She went to Seattle and telephoned from there. The doctor had closed his office and moved to California without leaving a forwarding address. Did I know of anyone else?

Some of the doctors who had been raided when I was had reopened, so I suggested she get copies of the July 6 newspaper for their names and call them one by one. She thanked me, and that case, I thought, ended there. But it did not.

Three days later she phoned again, sobbing so hard I could barely understand her. Finally, I was able to piece out her story. While she had been in the basement of her home—looking through old newspapers to find the July 6 edition—her mother had come upon her and demanded an explanation of her strange behavior. The girl broke down and told her about her condition.

Instead of sympathy and understanding, she got a rain of abuse and was ordered out of the house. Finally, exhausted from her tirade, the mother "relented" to the extent of allowing her to remain through Christmas.

I told her to come to me. She never did.

On the morning of Christmas Eve, I went to my attorney's office to discuss some matters connected with the coming trial, but I found it hard to concentrate. I was thinking of that young woman. Suddenly, I blurted out her story and before I could finish broke down crying. For the first time since I met him, the lawyer showed emotion and became more than an animated law book. He almost seemed to understand.

"You'd really give anything to help her, wouldn't you, Ruth?" he said.

"But I can't, I can't," I sobbed. "I don't even know her name."

I spent Christmas with my family, romped with my grandchildren, gave thanks for many blessings and tried to forget that woman. If only I could have helped her the first time, she pleaded with me. What heartache might have been averted.

Week after week of such importuning from other women made me more and more distraught. I could no longer ignore their cries for help. Despite the case pending against me, I reopened my clinic.

In the spring of 1952 came my first appearance in court. This was a legal move to seek suppression of the evidence taken from my office without a search warrant during the July 1951, raid. The court ruled in my favor and ordered the documents and other things returned. Some of them were but many instruments and photographs were withheld to be used as exhibits at the trial.

The trial opened April 28, 1952 and dragged on for eleven days. I was charged not with performing illegal abortions but a broader and certainly vaguer offense— "maintaining an establishment injurious to public morals." When the law is used, not as prosecution, there must be a resort to subterfuge.

A highlight of the lengthy courtroom session—and a pitiful one—came when Ann's mother was called to the stand. Already humiliated before her friends and identified in the newspapers and over the radio, she was now to face the probing of a zealous prosecutor.

When my lawyer asked Mrs. Kelly if she and her daughter had

been treated kindly at the clini...
asked if she was grateful, she bu...
what we would have done," she so...
us."

The Deputy District Attorney's fa...
rin. He scanned the jury, arose, appro...
and was granted an early recess. The...
witness when court reconvened, nor t...
days of the trial. And I would not permit... ...all her
back, although her testimony would ha... ...valuable to my
defense. She had suffered enough.

Naturally, I did not divulge the identity of the physician who
had sent the Kellys to the clinic.

The prosecution cited the 1864 law which made it a nuisance
to maintain an office, in a building or house, where an abortion
could be obtained. As it stands now, that law is an anachronism.
Like most of these legal relics, it does not take into consideration changes in customs, more and ethics that occurred in the
intervening years. The more than 100-year-old law may well
have been passed in a wave of outrage following the death of a
women who died from self-abortion or at the hands of an amateur abortionist. Yet such deaths occur today because trained
and experienced abortionists are hounded into retirement by
that very law.

In the trial preliminaries, the picking of a jury was of un-
ending interest to me. I smiled when the prosecutor began his
examination of a prospective juror, a pleasant little housewife,
asking her what she thought of abortions.

She spoke right up to him. "I think it's a woman's personal
business to decide whether or not she wants an abortion."

It goes without saying that she was eliminated from that jury.

Once the jury was empaneled, the trial went its dreary way.
There were tragic moments such as the appearance of Ann's
mother on the stand. And there were the exhibits, made to look
as gruesome as possible. It mattered not to the prosecutor that
a judge had earlier ordered to return of the things taken from the

arch warrant. The instruments and endless
ere placed into evidence.

he photographs brought one of the few periods of
elief in that long courtroom session. In order to appreci-
the irony of it, I must go back to the day of the raid.

A nurse in my clinch that day had prepared surgery for a
patient who complained of pain and soreness in the womb. To
relieve the soreness, the doctor was going to insert a medicated
tampon. The nurse had taken the instruments from the sterilizer and placed them in a white porcelain pan containing two
five-grain tablets of Lily's antiseptic Cyanide. The resultant solution was of pink color.

During the raid a newspaperman from the Oregon Journal had
spotted this pan and excitedly called for his photographer. He
had a picture of a story of a pan "full of blood" for his sensational
coverage. It mattered little that the patient for whom the instruments were being sterilized had not even entered the treatment room.

At the trial, the reporter took the stand and testified that
the antiseptic cyanide was blood. I remember thinking that the
best education for a reporter who doesn't know the difference
between antiseptic pink coloring and blood might be a stout
punch in the nose.

More seriously, it was strange to sit there in the courtroom
and hear the instruments in that photograph described as tools
for an abortion. The seized instruments presented at the trial
were a speculum, a tenaculum, a small gall bladder forceps and a
sound. The prosecutor kept hammering at the jurors that those
were the instruments I used in my trade. The jurors, none of
whom had even a smattering of medicine or surgery, apparently
gullible enough to believe this bizarre suggestion. Never did the
prosecution present a curette nor a dilator, the instrument usually associated with abortions.

I was also momentarily amused when the State of Oregon
called an expert witness to identify several small bottles of
drug samples seized in the raid. He said they meant nothing, and

he was right—the samples had been sent to Dr. Ed Stewart years before my pharmaceutical firms and hadn't been touched for years.

Then, the deputy district attorney handed the witness a small box. I gasped. They were the reducing pulls that had disappeared from the raid.

"Yes, I have analyzed these pills," said the expert witness. "They consist of vegetable coloring and starch."

Poor me. No wonder I had not lost any weight while taking them—and at $10 a box.

Such were the elements of farce in a trial where the verdict was a forgone conclusion. At one point, the prosecution even called a learned medical man who testified that an abortion could be performed by inserting a finger in the cervix and pressing down with force. Other physicians in the courtroom were bug-eyed when they heard this ridiculous theory. During a recess I heard one of them remark, "Some finger."

The whole trial didn't go against me. At one stage my attorney described me and my associates as "angels of mercy, helping girls out in their afflictions." He argued that it was a wholly legal to attempt to save a girl from an incestuous birth. "Did we outrage public decency and impair public mores as charged in the indictment?" he asked. "Who has been outraged? Was the doctor who sent her to the clinic outraged? Were her parents outraged?

On the sixth day of the trial a Longview, Washington Housewife dropped what the newspapers called a "bombshell" into the trial by testifying during cross-examination that not only had I talked one of her friends out of the idea of getting an abortion but that I had bought a layette for the child. For a brief moment in that trial I was made to look like a human being and not some kind of monster.

In his final argument, my lawyer declared that there were no denials by the defense that women had abortions at the Stewart Clinic. His further argument that these abortions were legal abortions, performed under proper circumstances fell on deaf ears.

The jury was out about two hours. Then is filed in with a verdict of guilty. A few days later, Circuit Judge Martin W. Hawkins sentenced me and a doctor in my employ to six months in the Multnomah County Jail at Rocky Butte. Two of my female staff each received three-month sentences. My attorney immediately gave notice of appeal.

CHAPTER FOURTEEN

So many things happen during a much-publicized trial that it is all but impossible to set them down here—and it is just as well that some of these things remain unwritten.

The notoriety caused by the sensational trial brought many attendant troubles for me. It was no secret that my practice had been lucrative in World War II and the post war years.

My income during the years of the Stewart Clinic was as much as $182,000 a year. I make no apologies for earning that kind of money. I worked hard for it and, as subsequent events have shown, I took tremendous risks for it. I paid staggering legal fees.

Furthermore, the nature of my business made me a target for both would-be extortionists and thieves. On several occasions during those years' burglars entered my home and made off with large amounts of money, none of which was ever recovered.

During the trial in the spring of 1952, I received a telephone call from a trusted woman friend who had received a call herself, from a stranger. She had made arrangements to meet this stranger—a woman we'll call "Mrs. X"—who offered "possible help" in my trial.

When my friend met with "Mrs. X" she was brazenly told that "Mrs. X" had control over some of the persons on my jury. "Mrs. X" was equally brazen in telling my friend that it would cost money to "fix" the jury. I told my friend, when she reported this, to go home and forget the whole thing.

The night before the case went to the jury the connivers were still at work. A man drove to my daughter's home, talked in circles for a time and then made the statement he could get me a "not guilty" verdict for $15,000. He went so far as to tell her she would have to "work fast," because he was "tired out from sitting up all last night plotting with some jurors."

My daughter was almost speechless with her indignation, but she managed to tell the man to come back in a few hours after she had talked to her husband. When the shakedown artist returned my son-in-law answered the doorbell. His remarks to the despicable character who had asked for the $15,000 were couched in a language you'll never hear on your TV set. A censored version of them was:

"My mother-in-law will take what the jury decides. You may be telling the truth about controlling the jury and you may not. Whichever it is, we want no part of it. Get going."

The man scooted for his car. Once inside, with the motor going, he yelled: "She'll be sorry." The only thing I've ever been sorry about was that my son-in-law hasn't booted him off the porch.

While my appeal on the misdemeanor charge was pending, the flow of distressed, frightened girls into my office continued. They came in tears usually but left with smiles.

Most of us know what is meant by "entrapment." My lawyers have tried to explain to me, over the years, how the law enforcement people can sometimes employ entrapment—the deliberate setting up of a situation to induce a person to commit a crime—but to me it is a despicable subversion of my understanding of the law.

One day, early in 1953, we were visited by a woman posing as a wronged girl in need of an abortion. With her was a male newspaper reporter posing as her brother. After the reporter handed some marked bills to the receptionist, the "patient" was escorted to a dressing room. The receptionist entered my office with the money. As she placed it on my desk, the phone rang.

I had difficulty placing the excited voice, that of a deputy sheriff whose wife I had once befriended. "Get everyone out of there, Ruth," he said. "The District Attorney's going to raid you again today."

I relayed the message to the receptionist who picked up the bills and handed them to the masquerading "patient." "Take this back," said my receptionist. "And get out, quickly. There may be some trouble and we don't want you involved."

The women refused the money, pretending not to understand. "I won't take it," she insisted. "I came here to be helped! I must be helped! Please hurry and take care of me."

"There's going to be a raid," the receptionist explained, "and we're trying to protect you. You don't want your name dragged through the courts, do you? You've got to leave quickly."

The "patient" laughed, reached inside her brassiere, and pulled out a handful of crumbled papers.

"I'm a policewoman," she announced, "and here are the warrants for everyone's arrest."

Then, she ran to a side door, opened it, and a squad of arresting officers trooped in. One again I went to the county jail, marched up the steps to be booked and released on bail.

The District Attorney had taken no part in the second raid on my clinic. I heard later that he was sitting on a stool in a small restaurant across from the courthouse. As we were marched up the steps, he was heard to say, "There goes Ruth Barnett. I hope I get my $300 back." He meant the money the policewoman posing as "Little Sister" had tried to pay me.

I reflected, long afterward, that I had some idea how he felt about the money. The police had seized $800 of my money in the first raid of my clinic. More than 16 years later I still wonder at times whether I'll ever get that $800 back.

CHAPTER FIFTEEN

After my second arrest it was time for a long, hard look at the future. I sat behind the desk in my office and faced a lot of facts, not the least of which that I was a 60-year-old woman with a pack of trouble on my hands.

I was momentarily due to go to jail on my 1952 misdemeanor conviction. I was under probation on a manslaughter by abortion charge and I would now most likely be adjudged in violation of the terms of that probation. And here I was under indictment on a new charge.

At the courthouse my lawyer had gone to see the District Attorney about reducing my bail. He had come back, slightly flushed, to announce:

"Ruth, the District Attorney is pretty angry. He feels you have let him down in re-opening your clinic wile your cases are still pending."

"He's angry?" I said. "How about me? He can feel any way he damn pleases. You tell him there are enough bastards in this world with mothers and fathers and I was trying to do the world a lot of good by preventing the other kind."

It was an intemperate thing for me to say and my lawyer was thoroughly shocked. He hustled me to the elevator and as the jail cage door was closing, I heard a young deputy say something that brought back my composure:

"There goes the cleanest-looking and nicest-smelling prisoner we've ever h ad.:

But once back in my office I forgot about such things as my perfume and thought about the obvious—my clinic this time would be closed and closed for good.

THEY WEEP ON MY DOORSTEP

The receptionist came in, hugged me, said a few words of encouragement and left. I listened to the click of her heels down the tile corridor. I heard the elevator door open and close.

I was alone in surroundings that had been a vital part of my life for twenty-five years. What could I do? I could not endure one raid after another. My persecutors were obviously remorseless and would not give up as long as it was to their advantage to invite the public with newspaper crusades.

I made a slow, retrospective journey through the rooms of my beloved clinic. There were various memorabilia of patients of years gone by. I was suddenly reminded of a patient who had haunted me for a long while. She was only 15, slightly build, blue-eyed, blonde and innocent with immature breasts poking small rounded points into her sweater. She seemed numb as I had questioned her. She said she had been raped.

"Who raped you," I asked.

"My father. He was drunk."

"When?"

"Maybe seven months ago."

Examination corroborated her statement. She had been pregnant too long. When I said that an abortion would be impossible, she asked, almost tonelessly:

"What can I do?"

"Nothing," I said. "You'll have to have the child."

"My own father's baby?"

I could only nod. My throat was too choked for speech. She arose, went to the door, stood there a moment, turned toward me as though she was going to say something further. But she said nothing. She was weeping. She shook her head once and left.

The next morning the police fished her body from the Willamette River. I remembered a poem I once memorized by Thomas Hood:

> "One more unfortunate,
> Weary of breath,
> Rashly importunate,

> *Gone to her death!*
> *Take her up tenderly,*
> *Lift her with care;*
> *Fashioned so slenderly,*
> *Young, and so fair!..."*

How many such unfortunates, I wondered, could have been spared ignominy or death if they had been able to avail themselves, in time, of a safe abortion? I could only guess.

I sat there that evening until long after dark, feeling more than a little sorry for myself, a whole lot sorrier for the girls I would no longer be able to help. Finally, I pulled myself together and went home.

Shortly after I left my offices that day another squad deputies from the District Attorney's office arrived at the darkened building, showed the superintendent a search warrant and got them to open my door. Apparently, all they were looking for was the plastic curtain used with my operating table. They got it.

The next morning, I arrived at my office with plans to start packing. My packing was postponed by a telephone call from the D.A.'s office. They had still another warrant for my arrest—this time on a misdemeanor charge. And—I could scarcely believe it—this time they asked me to drop by the courthouse to be served. After the much-touted raids with a veritable battalion of officers and reporters it was quite a change. "Come on over, girls," the officers said. "We want to book you."

There were a number of possible explanations for this rather odd change of pace, but I learned before long the real one. An effort had been made the night before to arrest us at home and take us to the jail at a late hour. This would have precluded us from raising bail before morning and we would have to spend the night in jail. But my friends in the sheriff's office didn't cotton to the idea. They were able to see to it that the deputies with the warrants "just weren't able to find us after dark." It was a nice gesture, particularly since both of us were in our homes and the addresses were on the warrants."

It was clear that I had another immediate problem and that was letting potential patients and those physicians who sent them to me know, once and for all, that I was no longer in business. To do this, I decided to call in a reporter from the Portland Oregonian. His name was Wallace Turner and he has since won a great many awards for his reporting. His stories, I thought, were always fair to me and ethical which was more than I could say for some of those who had written about me and testified against me. And he had never stooped to anything as low as the "Little Sister" act with which one of the reporters tried to frame me.

I telephoned Turner and arranged to meet him that afternoon. I spent a couple of hours giving careful thought to a press statement. The following day, this story by Turner appeared in the Oregonian:

"DR. RUTH BARNETT WILL CLOSE CLINIC"

"Dr. Ruth Barnett Tuesday announced closure of her Stewart Clinic and began vacating her eleven-room suite in the Broadway Building.

"'I have closed the Stewart Clinic,' the doctor said in an interview. 'I have completely discontinued all my practice. I am retiring from my life-long work, not from choice. Everyone who reads the newspapers knows why I am retiring.' Dr. Barnett pulled no punches in her interview.

"'I have been proud to own and run this clinic for many years,' she said. 'It is about 60 years old now. I bought it from Dr. Ed Stewart. The clinic units have always been as good as the best anywhere in Portland.'

"Nor did she attempt to talk around the type of practice which has been the chief business of the clinic.

"'We've always treated the women's diseases generally,' she explained, 'but much of the work we have done and much of the work done here since the clinic was started has been the performance of abortions. And a lot of it was on reference from other doctors.

"'About seventy-five percent of the abortion cases have been re-

ferred to the clinic by physicians and surgeons in Oregon and other states.

"'Leading gynecologists and obstetricians, many of them leaders in medicine, have regularly referred patients here for abortion they needed.'

"Dr. Barnett asserted that her acceptance by the medical profession was 'because of the skills, techniques and standards we've had here.'

"She said, 'Newspaper have not pointed it out, but the medical profession has recognized that many conditions require that abortions be performed.

"' The Oregon legislature has passed a law that says an abortion may be performed when the health of the mother is at stake,' she pointed out. 'There are a lot of social and religious questions involved, however, and I've always felt that an abortion should not be performed without a good reason.'

"She has turned down a lot of women, she said. 'I've spent a lot of hours talking young women into going ahead and having their babies.

"'Lots of times I have bought layettes for them in order to get them to agree that they would not leave my office and go to some other clinic.'

"But while she has retired from her abortion clinic, Dr. Barnett said she 'has many memories and I plan now to study and maybe write a book on the controversial subject of abortion.

"' Just about everybody agrees that there are two sides to the question. It could be that my experience in this field will help legislators as well as doctors and the general public to understand it all better.'"

That very night I began writing this book.

CHAPTER SIXTEEN

In March of 1954 the blow finally came, and it left me stunned. True, I had expected some sort of sentence—but not the two consecutive six months jail sentences handed me by Circuit Judge James R. Bain.

The newspapers seemed to think there was some kind of "deal." There was no such thing. Because of the constant harassment by the district attorney's office, I had decided to withdraw my appeal before the Oregon Supreme Court against the May 10, 1952 conviction on the misdemeanor charge. That accounted for one of the six months sentences. A 90-year-old law which made it an offense to operate a place where an abortion could be obtained. It was, it seemed to me as though I was going to jail for an offense in the same category a spitting on the sidewalk.

There was a second case in which I had pleaded guilty to a second count of operating an unlawful abortion business and a further count of "manslaughter by abortion." On the manslaughter indictment, Judge Bain postponed imposition of sentence for five years—an action tantamount to placing me on probation.

What the public didn't know about this new case—the newspapers never did print the story and it is told here for the first time—is that it concerned a woman who lived in horror, for good reason, of the prospect of having a second child.

Her name was Leona, her husband was overseas in Korea and, just the year before, she had given birth in a Vancouver, Washington hospital to a stillborn child, a baby born with its brain hanging outside the cranium in a sac. Small wonder that she dreaded the prospect of a second child!

Leona was working at the telephone company when she came to me in October of 1952. When I made an examination, I could see that there was a problem. My surgical glove came away bearing a putrid discharge. It was quite possible that the fetus was already dead. I agreed to do an immediate curettage.

On the operating table, Leona has an epileptic seizure. But after surgery she seemed well enough, asked for a cup of tea. While she was drinking her second cup, she began hemorrhaging. I took her back to the surgery and tried manual manipulation of the womb to stop the bleeding. Neither this nor any of the other usual remedies seemed to work. I could check the flow for a while, but then it would begin again. Her blood did not have any power to coagulate. She finally told us that she was a bleeder. "When I was a child, I cut my hand and my folks had to take me to the hospital to stop the bleeding," she said.

I had my own ideas about the nature of the bleeding. Over the years I'd become convinced that the coagulation of blood is connected with diet. I had noticed during the war, when some foodstuffs were in short supply, that women tended to bleed more freely. I believe poor coagulation is directly connected with vitamin deficiency, but just what had caused it in Leona's case wasn't important. Getting her to a hospital for a transfusion was.

I called the office of a Portland obstetrician, an old friend. He was out of the city, but one of his associates agreed to take care of Leona at Good Samaritan Hospital. I gave her $75, had my son-in-law pick her up in his arms and drive her to the hospital. My nurse went along with Dr.—'s patient.

At the hospital they did a dilatation and curettage. They may have found a little residue. Later, when I had an opportunity to read the pathologist's report there was a statement, they had found no placental tissue but that her blood was, indeed, lacking in platelets. They gave her four blood transfusions.

In three days, she was ready to leave the hospital. I called the business office and found out the amount of her bill. Then I called a friend, bought a "get well" card and put it in an envelope with two $100 bills. My friend took the envelope to her and she was most grateful. But I made the mistake of writing a little message on the card. There are informers in all hospitals and, ultimately, my act of kindness let to a new indictment against me. I doubt very much that the prosecutors who presented this case to the grand jury ever told the jurors about the baby born to Leona the year before with the brain hanging in a sac outside her skull.

The police never allowed Leona to come to see me again. I saw her, ultimately, in the courtroom. That was the day I made up mind to change my plea to the new charges to one of "guilty."

Before I changed my plea, the trial was actually underway. They spent several days empaneling a jury and I thought, at the time, I would rather take my chances with a firing squad than with that bunch of nitwits. Too often, the more intelligent citizens whose names are drawn for jury duty have jobs which keep them from serving or physicians who are able to "get them off." Most of the those who are left to serve are the ignoramuses.

I realized there are expectations, but sitting there, at the time, I couldn't help but wonder what difference it made to these people that "manslaughter by abortion" was a vicious and ridiculous law. How can anyone tell whether a fetus is alive or dead before the fetal heartbeat can be heard? Not all abortions are performed before it is possible to hear the fetus. Furthermore, the majority of women who came to me had already taken any of the thirty or forty different pills sold over the counters of drugstores. Such pills can sometimes kill an embryo but cannot expel it. There was no way Leona or anyone else could tell if the embryo in Leona's womb was dead or alive—and there I was, sitting there charged with manslaughter.

At that trial, too, it occurred to me how unfair the jury system and the method of selecting juries can be. The deputy district attorney kept impressing on each prospective juror the idea that "the law reads that the state protects the child from the moment of conception." Why not, I wondered, from the time of the first twinkle in the father's eye?

My lawyer was forbidden by law from asking venireman if they were of the Catholic faith. Because of the restrictions on such a question, he was forced to use subterfuges in his examination of the prospective jurors. "How many children do you have?" he asked a woman. When the woman said she had five we decided to challenge her peremptorily on the assumption she was a Catholic. Later, after she had been challenged and was off my jury, the same woman came over to me and asked me about a nurse who had worked in Dr. Stewart's clinic. The woman I had thought a Catholic, and therefore dangerous to me as a juror, turned out to be an old friend of Dr. Stewart's who had spent a great deal of time in his clinic. There was irony for you.

A juror dismissed by the prosecution turned out to be a man who had been having an affair with one of my patients —a woman who had been to me their different times for operations. And a woman accepted for a jury—one we thought would be friendly because she was employed by a good friend of mine—we later learned was rabid with her detestation of me and my practice. So much for the tricky business of selecting juries.

Anyway, I sat there watching the farce of jury selection played out. I watched the prosecution bring in its star witnesses—Leona and a nurse from Good Samaritan Hospital. I didn't want to embarrass Leona by looking directly at her, but I watched her from the corner of my eye. I saw her twisting a small, wilted handkerchief with a yellow border. I noticed that she had put on about twenty pounds since I saw her in October of '52. I had heard that she had given birth to a normal baby in December of '53, so my order for transfusions had apparently done some good.

As I watched her sitting there, twisting that handkerchief, I knew she hadn't had a Chinaman's chance. I, too, had been in grand jury rooms and I knew the pressures which could be brought to make a person talk. I felt no real malice for her.

What did concern me—and I had lain awake nights worrying

about it since the trial had begun on March 1—was the embarrassment that would be occasioned for the obstetrician who had treated Leona at the hospital. He could truthfully say he did not know me. But would his snootier patients ever believe this? Was there not a danger he would lose prestige in the Catholic hospitals where he practiced? Would there not be a widespread idea that he had come into the case just to help me? It was a heavy burden to place on a young doctor who had only been trying to help a bleeding patient.

Disturbed by the make-up of the jury, distraught over Leona's courtroom role and concerned about the young obstetrician, I made up my mind to tell my attorney's I would change my plea to guilty if they could get the District Attorney's office not to prosecute my associates. In that sense, I did try to make a "deal."

On the Monday morning when the jury was to begin hearing testimony the judge ordered the jury out while I entered the new plea. Manslaughter by abortion charges against my staff were dismissed, but as it turned out, they had to go to jail anyway. The misdemeanor case on appeal to the state supreme court was still against them.

After I was sentenced, the judge called the jury in and dismissed them. It seemed to me that both the jury and the gallery were a disappointed bunch of people. No chance to see Leona, frightened and cowering, twisting her handkerchief on the witness stand. No opportunity to observe the embarrassment of a prominent young doctor. No testimony from expert witnesses about such gruesome things as blood clots, pathological tissue and discharges. The morbidly curious had to content themselves with the afternoon newspaper's headline—"Ruth Barnett Pleads Guilty, Gets Year In Jail."

The judge, after sentencing me to the two six-month terms, gave me ten days in which to put my affairs in order. Even with this time, I found it hard to make the necessary adjustments of attitude. What should I wear, for instance? What does a woman wear when she goes to jail? What was I allowed to take with me? I didn't have any ideas how to answer such questions.

Business-wise, things were in pretty good shape. Some months before—when it became obvious, I could no longer do abortions—I had gone into a reducing clinic in association with Dr. Jesse B. Helfrich, a splendid physician and a brilliant pathologist. I had always had a tendency to overweight myself and I was seriously interested in problems of weight control. Through friends in Dallas, Texas, I had learned of a new drug which, under proper medical supervision, enabled a woman to lose a great deal of superfluous fat.

The Slim-U Clinic in the Alderway Building at SW 12th Avenue and Alder Street was though by many people to be some kind of "front" for my abortion practice. In fact, it was set up strictly for the purpose of helping men and women to lose weight. We had nearly as many men as women patients. We had our own laboratories, did basal metabolism and urinalysis.

The reducing methods we used depended heavily on accurate and frequent checks on the patient's metabolism and general physical condition. We used drugs and a diet, but the dieting was not strenuous. Although patients were encouraged to get a healthful amount of exercise, there were no exercises prescribed and no gym equipment or anything like that. I, myself, quickly lost 30 pounds under Dr. Helfrich's supervision. The idea occurred to me that I was still helping women with their problems. Not the serious problem of unwanted pregnancy, but with a problem which makes life burdensome for many women. It was a good business and it flourished.

At any rate, Dr. Helfrich and my other associates agreed to keep the reducing clinic open during my incarceration. We all got together at the clinic for a farewell dinner of Chinese food.

Right up to the eve of the day my sentence was to begin, I hoped against hope that Judge Martin Hawkins would relent and let my staff go free even though there was no hope for me. But he would not move an inch. It was an election year and the judges were all afraid of the newspapers. More important, he had his sworn duty to enforce the laws, no matter how unfair these laws might be.

So, on the evening of March 17th, 1954, a friend in the sheriff's office came to drive us to Rocky Butte jail. In those days it
was considered one of the nation's better such institutions, but
we weren't all that enthusiastic about testing its facilities. We
were a day early and the others thought we might as well wait
until the last possible minute before going to the jail. But I had
had enough of delays and waiting for the inevitable. "Let's go to-
night," I said, "and get this damnable business over with."

CHAPTER SEVENTEEN

It was the roll of dimes that finally brought home to me the nature of prison.

I must have had some idea that a jail was something like a hospital. If you wanted to call a friend, you just walked down a corridor and used a pay telephone—or so I thought. That's why I had brought the roll of dimes with me to Rocky Butte.

But in the warden's office they relieved me of all my personal possessions. The dimes were the last thing to go. "There isn't any telephone for the inmates, Ruth," said Jack Matthews, the head jailer. So, the nightmare began.

A matron led me to the dormitory. It was late and the lights had long been out. She showed me my assigned bunk and left. The room was quiet, too quiet. I knew there were supposed to be eight other women sleeping in that dormitory, but I sat down on the hard cot and stared into the darkness, thinking of my family, my friends, mostly about my four grandchildren.

Suddenly, the silence was rent by a woman's harsh whisper. "This is a kangaroos court!" she rasped. I heard movements in the room, made out dim shapes coming toward me. I was surrounded by a gaggle of giggling women. They ordered me to "stand trial" for breaking and entering a jail in the middle of the night," disturbing the regular guests.

When I recovered from the initial fright, I realized the kangaroo court proceedings were being conducted with mechanical good humor. But there was also a threatening undertone, I knew I had to go along with the farce. I was, naturally, found guilty. I was sentenced to share my few possessions with them—toothpaste, cigarettes, make-up and nighties. And I was forced to swear that I would never be a stoolpigeon.

At length, they tired of their game and went back to their bunks. I was exhausted. I stretched out on the cot and, with the cold comfort of the metal frame against my leg, fell asleep.

Next morning, I got a look at my dormitory mates. They seemed to be as ordinary as the women you might meet in a bus station or restaurant. But as I came to know them better, I realized they were not really ordinary.

There was a Jo Ann, for example, a quiet, demure Negro girl. Her common-law husband had abused her, threatened to cut her heart out. She had murdered him. There was Arms, part American Indian, who had arrived at Rocky Butte with a gun and knife in her suitcase. She had known the rules would not permit her to keep such weapons, but she had been told to "bring only what you need." Apparently, with her quarrelsome disposition, she had considered a knife and gun necessities. During my stay at the jail I was to witness a dreadful hair-pulling fight between the Indian girl and an inmate named Jean while the matrons just stood by and watched the battle.

Jean was in for stabbing a girl in a drunken brawl. Another dormitory resident was Diana, a prostitute and narcotics addict. There was Dixie, a shoplifter. There was a gal forger and a couple who were just "plain drunks."

These women inmates had one thing in common—something I was determined to avoid—an attitude of despair. Perhaps it was easy for me to eschew their negativism because my life had always had a purpose and meaning. But at times I found it difficult to rise above prison regimentation and the dull routine. Blessed with a sense of humor, I somehow managed.

My days swiftly fell into the required pattern. Breakfast at 7:30, then work. Luncheon at noon, then rest. Exercise in the yard on clear days. Dinner at 4 o'clock, a bath before bedtime, lights out at 10 p.m.

The food was plain, nourishing and dull, although probably as good as any other such institution. There were few spices and never any nutmeg. Herbs can be used to make a variety of concoctions and I suppose jail authorities have learned that, through experience.

Women prisoners were, naturally enough, equated with housekeeping duties. So, we mopped and scrubbed and polished. We sewed, mended, darned and patched. The matrons were, in the main, wonderful. The work, in the main, dismal. We did what had to be done. But sometimes we did it on our own terms. We exchanged chores. This probably sounds like a little thing to you, but it was a means of self-expression, a small display of personal decision and individualism.

I was able to keep my spirits up, and my weight down, with a rhythm system. When the dining room had to be cleaned, I had about twenty chairs to lift from the floor to the tabletops. So, I hummed a song with a measured beat, using chairs as weights. I swung into the chore as though it were my chosen exercise. I did the same with mopping, dusting, any job that had repetitions movements which I could set to a musical pattern.

This kind of tomfoolery helped, but it was not a cure-all. The idea of prison nauseated me. I failed to see what it could accomplish. It cages the body and beats down the human spirit. It had the overall effect of brutalizing and tearing down the dignity which man has tried so hard to develop.

From what I have observed, penal life does not prevent criminality but encourages it. An inmate can fraternize only with another inmate. Prisoners are kept in environments which can only nourish a hardening of the spirit and homosexuality.

Prisoners are outlaws, social outcasts. But Dixie was only eighteen. She was a docile girl who had given birth to five children by five different fathers. When she was caught shoplifting, she was stealing to feed her family.

According to law, Dixie had committed a crime against society. But surely, society was not guiltless. What about the crime of enforced poverty in a land of affluence and plenty? What about the crime of inadequate education in a so-called Age of Enlightenment? What about the crimes of society's indifference?

If Dixie was solely responsible for her crime, then it can only be that the five fathers of her five children are utterly irresponsible. And society, too, had shown a measure of irresponsibility. Why hadn't contraceptives and birth control information been made available to her? Why hadn't she been able to come to me —or another skilled abortionist—for our services?

If my experience with jail life has taught me anything, it is little more than a re-affirmation of my lifelong belief that good, decent, well-meaning people can, unconsciously, be capable of injustice to their fellow men.

The weeks at Rocky Butte went slowly enough. After my release, I heard the most ridiculous stories about how I had been given "special treatment" and that the jailer had been bribed to turn my county's prison into some kind of country club for my benefit. I even heard reports that I had been surreptitiously released from the jail from time to time in order to perform operations or to "live it up on the town." People have some quaint notions about the way their public institutions are administered.

In truth, Superintendent Matthews was a very kind man. He did everything he could to make prison life a little easier for me without breaking or bending any of his institutions' strict regulations. I remember him going to market to buy strawberries for us, for instance. He was a kind person who performed such little niceties. But when he occasionally brought us a special treat, it was something for all the women inmates, not just for me or those who went to jail with me.

Matthews did, after I had complained about the hardness of my bunk, find a softer mattress for me. I don't believe he should be condemned for making a prison cot a little more comfortable for a woman past 60. Believe me, his jail was still no bed of rose.

Strictly speaking, there was one little way in which the jailers may have turned a "blind eye" to one of my jail activities. I knew the girls liked to give each other permanents and it did a lot for their morale to have them. I charged quite a few home permanent kits to my account at the jail. There was little said about it, but one day one of the jail officers who'd been looking over the accounts remarked, "Mr. Ruth, you sure do go in for a lot of permanents."

Of course, every jail inmate learns something of the technique of "scrounging." It is part of survival and keeping one's spirits up during incarnation. What did I manage to scrounge by being friendly with a couple of my captors?—An occasional ice cream soda.

So, with lots of hard work and an hour or two a day spent making notes for this book, I passed the days at the prison we inmates called "Sunshine Terrace." Meanwhile, my lawyers was at work, doing his best to win me a parole. This became possible earlier than I had hoped when Circuit Judges Martin Hawkins and James Bain decided to invoke the "one-third time rule" used by the Oregon State Board of Parole. With five days off each month for good behavior, Judge Hawkins struck one month from the six months' sentence he had imposed, and Judge Bain, apparently acting in concert with Judge Hawkins, lifted the second six-months sentence.

On July 15, after 120 days at Rocky Butte, I came home to my lovely place in Portland's West Hills. There was a reporter and a photographer waiting for me. I was so nervous about being free again I couldn't open the lock of my front door. The reporter opened it for me, and I asked him and his friend inside the house.

"I have no grudges against anyone," I told them. That wasn't exactly the way I felt but being out of jail made me charitable.

I recall that I made a little joke about my works on this book. "It'll be very sensational," I promised them. "It won't be 'Love's Labor Lost,' I can promise you that." It was a silly joke, but I was suddenly feeling quite gay again.

After the story about my release appeared there were letters to the editor complaining about my sentences being cut short by the courts. On July 21 The Oregon Journal was moved to editorialize:

"*... We do not question the legal right of the courts to parole Dr.*

Barnett. That is established. But we do question the wisdom and property of the action.

"Dr. Barnett got off lucky. Too lucky, considering the nature of her crimes."

Those were harsh words and they stung, but I consoled myself with the knowledge that the newspaper reporters and editors really knew little of the facts. Maybe, when they finally read this book, they will understand something of the necessity of abortion.

Nor could the Oregon Journal have known the full cost of those 120 days behind bars. Among other things, the jail term cost me my last marriage. Earl Bush and I had been a highly compatible couple for many years. True, there had been some strain in our marriage for a time, but it was my incarceration that led to the final break. Shortly after my release we were to be divorced and I have not been brave enough to essay marriage since.

Meanwhile, I busied myself at the new clinic where Dr. Helfrich was working minor miracles with overweight men and women. My role in supervising the reducing programs was smaller than before I went to jail for a simple reason—the Oregon Board of Naturopathic Examiners had, while I was in Rocky Butte, revoked my licensed to practice naturopathy. Late in August I was forced to surrender the actual license to the district attorney's office. The revocation was because of my guilty pleas to the charge which sent me to jail.

In all the years since I lost my license, I have never made application for reinstatement. Most of my friends have continued to call me "Dr. Ruth." Even the vindictive newspapers have fallen so much into the habit of calling me "Dr. Barnett" that they stick with it. It matters little what anyone calls me—I answer to almost anything that's reasonably polite—as long as I can continue to do my work.

CHAPTER EIGHTEEN

Time and time again I have vowed never again to perform an abortion. And each time my resolve has been broken down by those who have come to weep at my doorstep.

So it was in 1954 when I came out of jail. Friends, lawyers, associates all hammered at me with the idea that I was under a probationary sentence and that if I were caught and convicted of another breach of Oregon's abortion laws, I would face a much stiffer jail sentence. They reminded me that I was no longer a young woman and even I—one who had fibbed about her age for so long she wasn't sure just how old she was—was aware that I had reached the August of my life. Like Emily Dickinson, I was fearful "lest this little brook of life some burning noon may go dry."

Former patients, many of them frantic, continued to importune me. My insistence that I had "retired" was met by tearful objections and entreaties for the names of other abortionists.

Sadly, I could not tell them "where to go." The same crusading newspapermen who had caused my arrest had closed down other abortion clinics. The few that remained in the Northwest were "underground." Inevitably, I began "sneaking" cases. At first, I took only the most desperate women with the most serious problems. But as the months went by I took more and more cases, practicing as much discretion as was possible.

My associates at the clinic were past masters of discretion. The woman who booked the patients, for instance, never allowed a patient to come to the clinic and be operated on the same day. And she developed a clever interview technique which made it possible to screen out those informers merely intent on entrapping me again.

If a woman said she had come from California by airplane, for example, my receptionist would ask her the time and number of her flight. It took only one simple telephone call to confirm that there was such a flight scheduled by the airlines. Other questions and the answers she received to them helped to buttress or destroy a potential patient's story.

There was a real need for such cloak-and-dagger precautions in the months after my release from jail. Periodically, while driving to an appointment or going shopping, I had the feeling of being followed. Several times, while walking, I was certain that a man or woman was shadowing me. There were strange calls at odd hours from people whose stories didn't add up. And there were the occasional visits from candid reporters who would say, "Come on now, give us the low-down on what you're doing."

I met such queries with general remarks about my retirement. But always there would be a skeptical look.

Eventually, the feeling of being followed and observed, like the visits from newspapermen, tapered off. I had ceased to be big news. The public lost interest in a mild-mannered grandmother who, to all intents and purposes, was busy finishing a book of memoirs and doing research on a social problem.

However, as my practice grew once more to large propositions it was inevitable, looking back, that I should be raided again. It happened in November of 1956 when a policewoman, posing as a "patient" managed, after three weeks of pleading and a trumped-up story about attempting to induce her own abortion, to get by my security screen and into my operating room. Once inside, she identified herself as a police "plant" and began screaming to a raiding party of police and medical examiners outside.

The events that followed were like a repeat performance of the soap opera played out a few years before. Dr. Helfrich, my receptionist and I were charged with conspiring to commit an abortion on the policewoman. The charges against Dr. Helfrich were later dropped for want of evidence. The physician had never played any role in my abortion practice.

There were, again, months of legal jousting. This time I hired Charles E. Raymond as my attorney. Formerly a district attorney he had played a role in harassing me. Now, he was to become my defender. He was a Catholic and a fine man versed in the subtleties of legal in-fighting. Like so many of the people who played major roles in my life story he, too, has gone on to join what Mark Twain has called "the majority."

Right after the 1956 raid, I closed down the Slim-U Clinic in the Alderway Building. Throughout 1957 and into the first few months of 1958 Raymond fought against the new indictments. The legal maneuvering seemed interminable. As fast as we would knock down one charge, the district attorney's office would come up with new charges. Finally, in March of 1958, my receptionist and I withdrew our earlier pleas of innocent to a fresh charge of manslaughter by abortion and entered pleas of guilty. Once again, I went before Judge Bain for sentencing. This time he gave me a stiffer jolt—one year in the county jail at Rocky Butte. My receptionist was given a sentence of six months.

A few days later I was again a guest of Multnomah Country at "Sunshine Terrace." Except that I was to be there 10 months in all (with time off for good behavior) instead of the four months I had spent there in 1954, jail life was not much different. Again, Superintendent Matthews was kind to me and the other women inmates. Again, there was the weary soul-destroying drudgery. Again I tried hard to keep my spirits up by making a game of it.

There were only a few bright moments in those ten long months. Once Superintendent Matthews took me out of jail to a dentist on N.E. Sandy Boulevard to have some dental work done. I guess that's what started more rumors that I could come and go as I pleased. I wish such had been the case.

Matthews did let me have a little extra allowance from my own funds at times to buy the other women ice cream sodas. And we had a few laughs when a couple of the gals, busy mending the prison clothes of the male inmates, got the bright idea of basting the legs and arms together with light stitching. We heard nothing about it for a few days and then Superintendent Matthews was suddenly there in a terrible temple, demanding, "All right, who's the wise guy?" It's surprising how knowledge of such a harmless prank helped me in some small measure to enliven the dreary days of prison life.

Sunday is visiting day at Rocky Butte and my daughter would often come to see me. Superintendent Matthews would let us visit in an office. My housekeeper came occasionally to see me, but mostly I would sit out in the recreation room and call the other girls for their visitors.

When you are in jail you don't live your own life, you live the lives of those around you. My friends and associates for those 10 months were narcotics addicts, prostitutes and hardened women criminals. But they were my friends, in a real sense. I played pinochle and canasta with them and we would lie around in the sun on the porch on the good days. I slept well and I lost weight.

I was always after Superintendent Matthews to give me a bigger allowance. I had to buy toothbrushes for the new girls who came in and combs and that kind of thing. He finally let me have an extra $2 a week which helped.

When visitors came and brought me candy, I would tell them not to bring a little bit of candy, but a lot of candy. There were 13 other girls their part of the time and we shared everything. That's the way it is with jail.

Visits from my attorneys helped to pass some of the time. My last husband, Earl Bush, had died and I was bringing a lawsuit involving his estate and some of his associates who were part owners of our former ranch in Eastern Oregon. We finally settled the matter out of court.

During this period the eyes of the country had been focused on Portland by the revelations of racketeering and ice operation witnesses who had appeared before the U.S. Senate's. McClellan Committee. An elected district attorney had been re-

moved from office and the governor of Oregon had appointed
Portland attorney Leo Smith as Multnomah County's acting district attorney. Smith was not only a stern man, but attorney for
the Catholic archdiocese of Portland. I knew from the beginning
of my incarnation that there was no real hope of my sentence
being commuted this time.

But the ten months finally came to an end and I was free once
again. You might think that this time, for good and all, I would
have given up my abortion practice. I had twice been to jail and
had been stripped of my license to practice. I faced serious penalties if ever arrested again. I had no clinic and little chance of
renting office space in Portland for a new clinic because of the
resentment felt toward me by a part of the community.

What did I do in 1959 when I was released a second time from
that grim rock-walled prison at Rocky Butte? I did what I had
been doing for more than 40 years. I went back to work, doing
what I knew best—helping women in trouble.

CHAPTER NINETEEN

The pace of my life changed quite dramatically after my second jail term. I suppose for every woman there comes a time when she must not only give in to the realization that the she is no longer young, must begin not only to think, but to l live like the grandmother that she is.

This transition for me was more difficult than for many women because I had a chronic slave to feminine vanity on the question of age.

I noticed the other day when reading through some old newspaper clippings that the newspapers gave my age as "49" at the time of my 1957 arrest. It doesn't surprise me. It was probably the age I had given them.

For eight years I was "28."

For ten years I was "49". The age 49 appeared on my driver's license throughout those 10 years.

Once, when I was arrested, an officer asked me my age for a form he was filling out. I asked him what age I had given on the occasion of my last arrest. He said I had given "50." "OK," I said, "make it 49." Every time I'm arrested, I take off a year."

When I at long last gave up the whole business of pretense with respect to my age I could scarcely remember just how old I really was. It became necessary or me to admit that I was an elderly woman because of social security and internal revenue requirements. But I'm a little sorry I finally gave in and confessed to three-quarters of a century.

You know, ever since I dropped that "49" from my driver's license and gave me real age my knees have hurt. I really believe that by pretending to be young a woman can help herself to stay young.

For eight years now, I have been very much the grandmother. I have taken several trips to Hawaii and bought a small condominium there. And in December of 1964 I was forced to come to grips with a disease which had taken a lot of my time and energy. But I get ahead of my story.

For more than six years I had no further brushes with the police, no harassment from police or medical examiners. There were several reasons for this.

While I was in jail in 1958, Charles Raymond was elected district attorney of our county. He was the man who had once prosecuted me as deputy D.A. and later defended me. As I mentioned earlier, he was a Catholic. But I had nothing to fear from him. It is the young, politically ambitious district attorney who hounds the abortionist. Mr. Raymond was a great man but a man who had come as far as he was to go up the political ladder. The DA's office was, to him, a step toward retirement, not the possibility of an even bigger swivel chair in the state capitol at Salem.

Another reason I was left pretty much alone by the authorities was that the Oregon public, sated by the endless sensations of the newspapers now engaged in a "vice probe" had pretty much lost interest in a woman who had been through the whole rigamarole of newspaper publicity, courtroom and jails several times. From a public interest point of view, I was a back number.

Perhaps a bigger reason was that my practice, once a large, well-organized clinical affair had been reduced by my arrests and the concomitant circumstances to a "back stairs" sort of clientele. Ironically, I was forced to adopt tactics of which I would have once been ashamed. I would pick up cases—and only the most desperate ones—and drive them to my own home where I did examinations and operations. Quantitatively, my practice was only a shadow of the once busy round I had known at my respective clinics.

Finally, and somewhat paradoxically, there was obviously a slight but inexorable shift in mass public opinion concerning abortion.

With the '60s came a great deal of public enlightenment on many social issues. Articles began to appear with increasing regularity in national magazines advocating a change in attitudes toward abortion. Several prominent Catholics found the courage to speak out against church dogma on the question. A few people even had the intestinal grit to suggest that those of us in the abortion business might be benefactors of the women in trouble rather than racketeers.

The new Colorado statute was not to come for several more years, but leading psychologists, sociologists, lawyers and others were pointing the way to attitudes less medieval. I was encouraged not only to continue my work but actually to hope that I might perform operations one day in the respectable atmosphere of complete legality. I vowed that if Oregon should revise its abortion statutes, I would seek relicensing by the Board of Naturopathy.

But such wishful thinking was little more than that in the early part of this decade. There was still trouble ahead for me, but I had become inured to trouble. My work was what mattered most, and I went ahead with it. I also found time for my grandchildren and their problems. Furthermore, old woman that I had become, I still managed to let my hair down occasionally at parties and at the nightclubs. You don't teach an old gal like me a new way of life even in what the newspapers call the "golden years."

If I have developed a more serious side to what has always been essentially a lighthearted nature, it is because I become concerned with the whole historical and sociological question of abortion. More and more I found myself studying some of the deeper aspects of the problem. And without making this book sound like a text—goodness knows, I make no pretensions to real scholarship—I would like to share with you just a few of the things I learned in the next few chapters.

CHAPTER TWENTY

Precisely at what moment does human life begin?

Throughout man's history the question has been debated, along with questions as to where and low.

Centuries ago it all seemed so simple for, in Genesis, it is written that God said, "Let us make man in our image, after our likeness..." It said nothing about a man being made from the sperm, the ova or a union of the two.

There was growing puzzlement for dedicated believers when, in 1651, the anatomist William Garvey wrote that "the eff is the common beginning for all animals," in 1672 when the surgeon Reinier de Graaf discovered follicles of the ovary and when a retired draper, Antony van Leewenhoek in 1675 saw with his own eyes, through the first crude microscope, those little "animalcules" which we call sperm.

The idea of preformation was still secure. Controversy raged not around that but as to *where* tiny, preformed man began his growth. Those who argued for preformation in the ova were known as ovists. Their opponents, who asserted that man were preformed in the sperm were known as the spermists and they had artist's drawings to prove it—outlines in which they depicted in the bulbous head of the spermatozoon the tiny man, squatting knees-to-chin in the approval fetal posture.

This quaint conceit stemmed from the age-old belief that Adam's body contained, in preformed miniatures, the entire human race from Genesis to Armageddon. And nothing dies more slowly than gospel truth of that kind.

About this time a "physick" sought to support the believe of the Immaculate Conception with a wonderful machine with which he had captured "floating animalcula" from the air. He maintained that these captured "animalcula," viewed under the microscope, were clearly little men and little women. He wrote a paper called "Lucina sine Concubitu" in which he pleaded for the innocent virgin impregnated by the very air she breathed. He went so far as to urge the British Royal Society to abolish copulation for one year, not only to prove the validity of his claim but to end venereal disease as well.

Arguments among men of science grew space. Big people grew from babies and babies few from tiny people, but where did these tiny people begin? In the ova or in the sperm? Or in the air? The controversy continued until 1854 when, under magnification, a sperm was seen entering an ovum. It was only the egg of a frog, but that was the end of the homunculus theory and the acceptance of the cell theory, by scientists, if not by theologians.

You see, if there is no preferred little man or little woman, who can term the act of abortion murder? And yet, a modern-day priest asserts that abortion is a "kind of lynching in the womb" and that it turns the mother's uterus "into a butcher shop." The idea of homunculus, the "little man," dies hard.

Modern biology tells us that the male sperm fertilizes the ovum and it is a single cell, a zygote, which gradually divides into more smaller cells which grow and develop through cell specialization. The fertilized ovum moves slowly through the Fallopian tube and into the uterus or womb. Here, it attaches itself to the uterine wall. About a week after fertilization it is a cluster of small cells called a morula, from the Latin word for "mulberry" which it resembls.

By the fourth week, it had developed a set of "gill arches" and a pronounced tail. It is somewhat less than one-third of an inch long. It has a heart. But what is it? Fish, flesh or fowl?

Until about the eighth week, it is generally referred to as an embryo, from a Greek word meaning a full or swollen egg. But as bone slowly replaces cartilage, it gradually assumes a recognizable form. It is then alluded as the fetus, from the Latin word for the formed unborn young of an animal.

When it is born it is, of course, a baby. And it seems obvious to me that a baby is something quite different from a zygote, or a morula, or any other unrecognizable, infinitesimal bit of matter.

The theologian uses the blanket term of "baby" or "human life" for the entire period of gestation. I would question his ability to identify the human embryo from that of any other animal.

Writing in Redbook magazine in May of 1967, Dr. Garrett Hardin, professor of biology at the University of California in Santa Barbara made out of scientist's case for abortion, tackling the question of when does human life begin.

Dr. Hardin said that only in the last 15 years have scientist come to know that in the nucleus of each living cell is a special kind of "information." This nuclear information is concentrated in the chromosomes in a giant chemical molecule called "deoxyribonucleic acid" or DNA for short.

"With only minor exceptions," wrote Dr. Hardin, "all the information needed to produce an adult man or woman is found in the tiny bit of DNA enclosed within the nucleus of a fertilized egg. Tiny?... The DNA needed to specify all the world's present population of 3.5 billion people weighs only one-seventeenth as much as single postage stamp."

The biologist said the zygote, which contains the complete specification of a valuable human being, is not a human being and almost valueless. Scientific studies show that at least 38 percent of all zygotes produced are spontaneously aborted. He ruled the loss of these, even at the fetal stage, at very nearly zero. The aborted fetuses are mostly defective, so there is truly a human gain. Even not defective, the human loss, he said, was negligible.

"A set of blueprints is not a house; the DNA of a zygote is not a human being..." stated Dr. Hardin. "The blueprints of the zygote are constantly replicated and incorporated in every cell of the human body. But there is no moral obligation to conserve DNA

—if there were, no man would be allowed to brush his teeth and gums, for in this brutal operation hundreds of sets of DNA are destroyed daily."

It is a favorite argument of those who oppose abortion that if "Beethoven's mother had had an abortion" we would have been deprived of his symphonies. Dr. Hardin says we could just as relevantly ask, "What is Hitler's mother had had an abortion?" Each conception is unique, but the expected potential of any absorbed fetus is exactly that of the average child born.

"A human female at birth has about 30,000 eggs in her ovaries. If she bears only three children in her lifetime," asks Dr. Hardin, "can we meaningfully say that mankind has suffered a loss in those other 29,997 eggs? (Yet one of them might have been a super Beethoven!)"

CHAPTER
TWENTY-ONE

The Catholic Church has been the bulwark of America's archaic abortion laws for centuries. In the past year alone, the Catholic clergy, buttressed by gynecologists and other physicians of the Catholic faith, have successfully fought reform legislation which would have liberalized abortion statutes in more than a dozen of the United States.

Colorado, late in April of 1967, became the first of the 50 states to legalize abortion—at least on three principal medical grounds. The new Colorado law makes abortion legal when a pregnancy has resulted from rape or incest, when pregnancy threatens serious consequences for the mental or physical health of the mother or when there are strong indications that a pregnancy may mean the birth of a baby with severe medical or physical defects.

My own state of Oregon had two abortion bills before the 1967 session of its legislature. One was similar to the new Colorado law and the other was a bill which would make abortion legal in any case of pregnancy where it was performed by a qualified practitioner. Both bills, fought hard by Catholic doctors and clergy, died in committee without a vote of the legislature.

Let it be known that I am a respecter of those who practice the Catholic religion, just as I trust I am those who practice other religious faiths. I do not quarrel with anyone else's beliefs. But I have believe a case can be made—any many intelligent Catholics have agreed with me—that the church's attitudes towards abortion have varied in past history, are not always consistent and can, like other elements of Catholic dogma, be changed to meet man's increased enlightenment and changing social conditions.

Tertullian, a Roman who converted to Christianity about 190 A.D., was an early influence in the Christian Church. He had studied the writings of Plato and Aristotle and had absorbed some of Greek philosophers' ideas about the pre-existent independence of the soul or mind. He remained, however, untouched by their permissive attitudes toward abortion.

Tertullian was also a student of the works of Philo of Alexandria who had lived in Rome about 40 A.D. Philo had condoned abortion because, in accordance with the teaching of Aristotle, the embryo becomes alive after 40 days, if male, and after 80 days, if female. Tertullian, however, flatly condemned any prevention of birth as being "premature murder." He maintained that the future man is a man already with the "whole fruit present in the seed." And he held the heretical view of the Traducianist that the soul is transmitted by the parent. This meant that the soul was present at the moment of conception.

Not so, said the Creationists, who disagreed. Their evidence was Genesis 2:7, in which "man became a living soul" only after he had received the "breath of life." As the text stated, man had received this breath not from any earthly parent, but from "the Lord God."

Tertullian developed the dogma of illicit abortion which is currently upheld by the Catholic Church. But Tertullian, perhaps unconsciously, made a basic error. Students of theology tell me that he was unacquainted with Hebrew and relied on a mistranslation of Exodus xxi: 22. This passage is the foundation for the Church's Biblical stand against abortion.

For some reason, Tertullian resorted to the Greek Septuagint version of the Masoretic Hebrew Bible. This differs from the later, more accurate vulgate Latin version. For example, the original Hebrew read "injury or no injury" which is "iniura" or "non iniura" in the Latin. The Septuagint version read "shaped or not shaped" which is "formatus" or "nonformatus" in Latin. There is an entirely different sense embodied in the two interpretations and Tertullian chose the latter. From that, he went on to refer to the "animate" or "inanimate" fetus when, in truth, the Hebrew referred only to the "injured" or "unharmed" mother.

The basis of the oft-used theological proof of fetal life lies in the Latin word "anima." As with its Hebrew counterpart, this Latin word means "breath." As such, if the fetus, or embryo, is "animate," as Tertullian originally propounded, then it should be able to breathe, if we fall back on the true meaning of "anima." But, biologically, we know the fetus does not breathe for itself while in the womb. It starts to breathe air only after it emerges and when, if necessary, the baby's respiratory system is activated with a vigorous slap on its bottom. If we use the true meaning of "breath" to translate the Latin word "animates," then the fetus is "inanimatus" and not possessed of its own breath of life.

This Tertulian error was continued into the 4th Century and was repeated by Jerome, who knew Greek, as well as Hebrew, Latin and Aramaic. He was even outspokenly aware of the "mistakes introduced by inaccurate translators." Yet, although his translation of the Hebrew Bible into the vulgate Latin version was more accurate than the Septuagint, he perpetuated Tertullian's interpretive errors in regard to the notions about the "animate" fetus.

In the 9th Century, there was some easing of the strict view with the Frisian Code. Abortion was still deemed reprehensible, but only infanticide was punishable. In the 10th century, the *Lex Ripuariorum* decreed that anyone who performed an abortion, before the fetus could be baptized, was to be fined 100 soldi. In the 11th Century's *Edictum Rutharis*, however, no such fine was made if the abortion was approved of by the woman, her husband, or the nearest male relative.

In 1148, with the publication of the *Decretum* of Gratian, there was yet another change of attitude, Gratian, a St. Felix monk of Bologna used Tertullian as his authority. According to Gratian, when the embryo was "informatus" (unformed), its removal by abortion was to be considered as being only a minor crime, an offense deserving of a fine. But if the fetus were to be "formatus" (formed), then the Biblical eye-for-an-eye punishment was to be imposed. The person responsible was to be put to death because a pre-natal human being had been denied baptism and so was cosigned to hell.

This Gratian doctrine was incorporated into the first, section of the Vatican's official *Corpus Juris Canonici* which, to this day, is in use as the Church's source of juridical law.

It is, however, not the only source.

Albert Magnus and St. Thomas Aquinas both maintained that what is called the "soul" enters the embryo after conception, only when there is sufficient physical form to receive it.

Pope Innocent III proclaimed, in the 13th Century, that abortion of a "foetus animates" was homicide, although abortion is of a "foetus inanimatus" was not.

Scholars are generally agreed that until the end of the 16th Century with the reign of Pope Sixtus V, the Church did, indeed, permit the termination of pregnancies within 40 days of conception for a male and 80 days for a female—the old Aristotelian concept.

Sixtus V in his papal bull "Effraenatum" defined all abortions as homicide, but after his death Pope Gregory XIV in another bull, "Sedes Apostolica," re-defined the matter, declaring that abortion was illegal only after a quickening of the fetus—and punishable by excommunication.

By the 18th Century it was the considered opinion of St. Alphonus Liguori, Doctor of the Church, that, "They are wrong who say that the fetus is animated at the instant of conception."

It was not until 1869 that the Catholic Church, under Pope Pius IX, reverted to the 16th Century position of Pope Sixus.

As I said, I am no student of theology nor even of history, but my reading and discussion with friends of the Catholic church's position seems to bear out the indisputable fact that there is both contradiction and a great deal of uncertainty in the church's various proclamations.

There is a canon law which states: "Non est homicida qui abortum procurat antequam anima corpora est infusa." (It is not homicide to procure abortion before the soul has entered the body.) Canon law also decreed that, if a woman were to be aborted in the first 40 to 90 days after conception, during the vegetative period, she was to be penalized with only a minor punishment, such as a pilgrimage to a holy shrine or a year's recitation of penitential prayers. But abortion of the fetus, after 90 days, could bring the woman a whipping, long imprisonment, deportation and even death, depending on the length of the pregnancy.

In the early days it was the aborted woman who was punished. Nowadays and ever since I began my practice and before, the threat of punishment is aimed at the abortionist, not the patient.

Behind the Catholic injunction against abortion there is obviously the belief that the real sin is depriving of the fetus of baptism and not the murder of the physical body of the fetus.

However, somewhat contradictory I would think, is the fact that Catholic priests do not, ordinarily, give a fetus the usual extreme unction or burial services afford a still-birth. It seems to me that this kind of differentiation, in practice, is at variance with their beliefs. If they do consider the fetus to be alive, why do they deny it the extreme unction given the child born dead? I have never heard this question answered.

Outside the Catholic church there has been somewhat different history of attitudes concerning abortion. The early Anglo-Saxons did not consider it illegal. Although Henry Bracton, in the 13th Century, declared that abortion was homicide, English law, generally, thought of it only as being a serious offense.

In the 16th Century, Sir Edward Coke denied Bracton's denunciation of abortion as murder. Coke is considered by man to have been the greatest of all English common lawyers. As one of the early champions of individual liberty, and as one of the early challengers of the so-called divine right of kings, he held that abortion, after quickening, was only a misdemeanor. Before quickening, it was no crime.

Abortion before the fetus quickened was not regarded as a crime in England until 1803. After that time, all abortions were redefined, legally, as homicides. This brought the law, medicine, even theology, back to the ancient days of Tertullian when the "fruit" and the "soul" were "in the seed."

Hippocrates, considered the Father of Medicine, has taught that life began 30 days after conception for males, and 42 days after conception, for females.

Galen, one of the honored physicians and medical writers of his day, adhered to the contention that both males and females had life 40 days after conception. This was part of the civil law among the early Romans.

Thomas Aquinas held that life was evidenced by acts of knowledge and movement. These basic actions were, to him, the first principle of the soul and he defined the beginning of life in the same terms.

The elders of Islam announced that life in the womb begins 180 days after conception.

Sir William Blackstone, who introduced English law courses to British universities which had previously taught only Roman law, agreed that, in the eyes of the law, life begins with the quickening of the fetus.

Theologians, philosophers, men of medicine and the men of the law have held their conflicting theories and arguments down through the centuries. But the fact remains that in most American states, even to this day, abortion continues to be regarded as a serious crime, punishable (as I know so well) by confinement to prison.

CHAPTER TWENTY-TWO

Abortion is as old as recorded time. Early historical accounts are studded with references to the use of both abortive drugs and instruments.

The Chinese Emperor Shen Nung (c. 2737-2696 B.C.) wrote a medical treatise which included detailed instructions. Inscribed with lacquer on strips of bamboo, the Emperor's recipe alluded to the use of *shuh yin*, known to us as mercury and as an abortifacient. The same abortifacient is prescribed in 1180 A.D. by the Chinese herbalists T'ang Shen-wei, who quotes from Emperor Shen Nung. Hence, techniques for abortions are at least 4600 years old and most likely even older.

Because of their dread of morganatic marriages, the early Egyptian royalty sometimes perpetuated their line through incestuous relationships, brother marrying sister. Harem concubines, however, were abundant and to make certain their illegitimate royal-commoner offspring would not day assert claims to the throne the Egyptians practiced abortion.

In Assyria, King Ninus' royal spouse, Semiramis, in the 9th Century, B.C., insisted on the attendance of the court physician when she accorded the king his marital rights, so that she could take the waters of the Nile, together with abortifacient herbs, to readjust any "accident" that might occur.

Even the redoubtable Amazons, female warriors who went so far as to have their left breast excised to accommodate the drawing of a bow-string and professed to despise men were known to become pregnant. To avoid being retired from battle as casualties of such dalliance, they would avail themselves of a specially-assigned woman warrior whose duty it was to "remove the sickness of bearing a child."

One reason given to account for the fall of the Roman Empire was the decline in the birth rate with a consequent alarming fall in population. Between the year 1 and 14 A.D., Emperor Augustus made a census which revealed that for every child born, 11 had been aborted. In Rome, for example, one neighborhood housed 39 abortionists whose services were used by the swarming meretrices or harlots of the area. If a harlot refused to undergo abortion, out of fear of pain, permission would be granted for her to bear the child, but only with the understanding it would become the property of the brothelkeeper who rear it to be a prostitute or pederast.

When archaeologists in 1748 uncovered the volcanic ruins of Pompeii among the colored frescoes revealed on a wall was one depicting the story of abortion.

In 1780, John Graham, an enterprising young Englishman, erected a Temple of Health in which he sold medications guaranteed to return his women clients to "a hitherto condition of chaste purity." His most popular treatment was given on a "celestial bed," an item of furniture with swivel-joint castors designed to shake the embryo loose from its uterine moorings.

Among the many mistresses of King Louis XIV were those tolerated by the royal advisors on the condition they avail themselves "of the services of a skilled midwife each double fortnight." Such abortion practices eliminated male hears who might lay claim to the throne of France.

In a book called "The Nether Side Of New York," one Edward Crapsey in 1872 described sporting houses in which "French-pill" were sold by resident abortionists. Another New York, muckraker, Gustav Lehning, in 1873 published, "The Dark Side Of New York" in which he described a veritable pleasure dome replete with 200 "female companions" and four residents' physicians who, in addition to their other duties, performed necessary abortions.

In olden days, attempts to discharge an unwanted embryo were sometimes made by giving a woman sneezing powders. Inserted into the uterus were pessaries containing such substances as galbanum and turpentine mixed with oil of roses and cypress.

Arab physicians prescribed such abortion techniques as bleeding, fasting, irritating the cervix with a quill, a piece of wood or a roll of paper, or by inserting ammoniac Linn, myrrh, juniperus sabina and other vegetable derivatives, some taken internally, and others applied into the vagina as irritants. A common practice was to open the cervix with muscle relaxing pessaries and then insert the uterus pads of wool dusted with irritant powders.

History tells us that the Hindu physicians used abortifacients extracted from various herbs and the ancient Greeks and Romans used such things as saffron, among other medications. According to Aetius, abortions were performed among Romans by binding the abdomen, shaking a pregnant woman violently, by injecting astringents into the uterus, by baths and by a whole pharmacopoeia of oral medications.

The Germans of the 17th Century believed that an abortion could be accomplished if the pregnant woman inhaled smoke from a fire made of dried ass's dung. Another method was for a pregnant woman's breasts to be suckled by another woman. In their ignorance, women of primitive tribes all over the world have resorted to weird practices to induce abortion. Manual methods of kneading the abdomen and compressing it are still being used by natives of Mbaya in Africa and by the Eskimos in Alaska. In Greenland, a length of wood designed originally for stretching wet footgear is inserted into the uterus. Eskimo women of Smith Sound in northern Canada use a whip handle or insert a sharpened walrus rib to puncture to membrane.

The Kroe women of Sumatra still apply hot stones to the abdomen, after swallowing the yolk of an egg laced with a strong fermented drink. Among the same people, medicine men have known to shoot tiny bamboo arrows into the uterus with a blow-fun to affect an abortion. Women in New Guinea jump out of trees to rid themselves of unwanted embryos. In Persia, hooks, abdominal beatings and even leeches are employed in attempts at abortion.

There are practices in some tribes, particularly among Australian aborigines, which I do not care to set down here. It is not my purpose to shock the delicate reader with bizarre detail of primitive surgical method, but merely to show that woman is not only long-suffering, but ever determined to rid herself of unwanted pregnancies, employing some highly ingenious methods in her attempts.

Over the centuries, four basic methods have been used to induce abortion. These could be categorized as chemical, physical, mechanical and surgical. I do not include magical rites which might accompany any of the four.

The use of chemicals, either orally or through application is very old. These drugs, used externally, are supposed to act as either as purgatives which irritate the intestines and pelvic areas or as stimulants to act as toxic poisons which will affect the embryo. Such methods ordinarily do harm, not good. They can cause excessive pain, bring on the loss of a great deal of blood and, often, burn the delicate tissues and leave open ulcers. The embryo is seldom affected. Many unfortunate victims of these crude attempts have become infected and have died.

The combination of chemicals and mechanical means can also be disastrous. Chemical solutions of soap, vinegar, salt, etc. may be introduced into the womb by means of a douche bag or syringe. In this way, air under pressure may be forced into the womb. Such an accident can wind up with a fatal air embolism.

Physical methods of abortion are born of woman's desperation. They include such acts as deliberately falling downstairs and riding horseback excessively. Women have impaled themselves on sticks implanted in the ground and bound their abdomens tightly with ropes or sashes. They have dropped heavy boulders on their bellies or had their pelvic regions stomped by others, even by animals.

When these physical means proved ineffective, women have often resorted to mechanical methods. They insert various, sharp pointed objects into their vaginas and through the cervical opening the womb. Button-hooks, rusty nails and, all too commonly, the wire of a straightened coat hanger have used for these highly dangerous practices.

Ignorant women and would-be abortionists who prey on ignorant women cling to the erroneous and always hazardous theory that the only requirement in producing an abortion is to place a foreign body into the womb. This, they imagine, will induce the womb of some kind of pseudo-labor, allowing the muscular contractions to expel the embryo.

Sometimes in all this accumulation on nonsensical folklore, someone recognized the inherent danger in a bare wire. This led to the use of a rubber catheter tube which is frequently threaded into the tube until, perhaps, its end becomes emplaces in the womb. A steady hand and sterile instruments are obviously required, at the very least. Either is seldom present. The results, more than often than one cares to think about, are perforated wombs, monstrously damaged tissues and, occasionally, punctured intestines. Excessive bleeding, infection and death are attendant possibilities unless adequate medical care is promptly available.

Even in this age of supposed enlightenment, women know very little about the facts of pregnancy and abortion. Whoever is responsible for "sex education" in this country, be it the schools, health departments, medical societies, responsible parents or whatever has apparently fallen down on the job. It is hard to believe that in this modern-day women will still put their faith in such things as crochet hooks.

The truth is that most methods used by women seeking to abort themselves are, at best, useless and, at worst, extremely dangerous. Falling downstairs and frantic horseback riding avail a pregnant woman nothing. If it worked for "my brother's wife's cousin," chances are that she wasn't pregnant at all.

Drugs and other chemical substances are almost always of no

value because they cannot reach the walls of the uterus where the embryo is situated. Even "shots" such as progesterone and prostigmine are of no effect in aborting a pregnancy. All they may do is bring on menstruation when it has been delayed by a cause other than pregnancy.

And yet, women since the beginning of time have, in their desperation and ignorance turned to desperate measures which have rarely done anything for them but compound their problems.

It is a pity when modern surgical abortions techniques have made the termination of early pregnancy a relatively safe and simple procedure.

CHAPTER TWENTY-THREE

There are two general types of abortions. One is spontaneously induced by the body for some physiological reason. It would appear that the body contains a sort of homeopathic mechanism sensitive to bodily changes. And if the woman is unable to produce a viable fetus during the fetal stage of five or six months a spontaneous abortion often results.

Many are the reasons for such spontaneous abortions: endocrine gland and thyroid deficiencies, hormone imbalance, nutritional lacks, diseases such as pneumonia and measles, syphilis, uterine fibroids, etc. Statistically, one out of every 10 conceptions abort spontaneously. And about 25 per cent of these are aborted in the first month of pregnancy without the woman even being aware of it.

Obviously, abortion is, or can be, a natural means of curtailing the birth process when the result could be either an unviable baby or an impaired or dead mother.

The second kind of abortion is that induced, not performed by the body but an external source. This source can be the pregnant woman herself (always a dangerous practice because of the lack of safety controls), an amateur friend or phony (also highly dangerous) or a professional physician. But most often these induced abortions—an estimated 1,000,000 a year in the U.S alone—are done successfully and safely but illegally, by processional abortionists such as myself.

Women seek out abortionist for a wide variety of reasons. In my 50 years of practice I have found that women seeking termination of pregnancy fall into the following categories:

1. Relatively young, married women who, already, have more children than they and their husbands feel they can afford.
2. Married women, past 40, who already have large families and are either too weary or too poor to take on additional burdens.
3. Childless married women past 40 who fear both the rigors of childbearing in their later years and the responsibility of caring for a child in their middle years.
4. Married women with sterile husbands or whose husbands have been away overseas. Hundreds of such women came to me during the Korean War.
5. Women are divorcees or widows Such women believe the encumbrance of a child would tend to limit their opportunities for remarriage.
6. Unmarried women, including young girls.
7. Women, usually married, who have had difficult birth experiences in the past and feel they cannot endure them again.
8. The women who have already given birth to defective children and who have been warned by doctors against further pregnancies.

Fear is underlying factor for virtually every woman who ever came to me for an abortion. Until very recently, the unwed mother has feared the dishonor, the disgrace and social stigma attendant upon bearing an illegitimate child. Even today there is still an element of social penalty for the unwed mother.

Fear motivates the married woman who is afraid she will be unable to provide for a new baby. It affects the thinking of the married woman who is concerned about losing her husband to "another woman" and believes pregnancy will make it harder for her to hold her man. There are women with dreadful fears of death in childbirth. And there are the women will "baby blues" who exhibit a range of fear symptoms all the way from explosive panic to suicidal tendencies.

It is fears, such as these, that often impel women toward an abortion. Such fears can be eradicated by abortion. And let us not think that such fears are always fanciful. Usually they relate to things that are very real: poverty, fatigue, loneliness, ostracism.

Modern, surgical abortion in the first three months of pregnancy is done by a technique known as curettage, a scraping of the womb to remove the embryo. After considerable thought, I have decided not to discuss the actual techniques involved in this book. This is not a textbook. Furthermore, there is always the danger that some desperate and foolish couple might attempt to use such information if it were printed here. The procedure is simple enough, but only in skilled hands.

There are, of course, a number of techniques for performing an abortion, most of them involving dilation of the cervix. In my discussions of abortion with gynecologists I have learned that my techniques, learned primarily from the late Dr. Watts (and not involving dilation; I've never owned a dilator) are markedly different in some respects from those in use by the medical profession. Some doctors have expressed amazement when they learn how simple I have made the basic procedure. A very few have scoffed and expressed doubt when told of my techniques. But even among the scoffers are those who have continued to refer patients to me over the years. It is hard to deny the skill of a practitioner who has never, in 50 years, lost a patient, never perforated a womb.

Just a word about those contemptible back-alley abortionists who prey on women, taking advantage of the reluctance of professional doctors to perform abortions—the characters who use instruments and techniques far beyond their competence and under filthy conditions. I have nothing but contempt for them.

Yes, I believe in completely legal abortions—as well as legal tonsillectomies and legal appendectomies. But I believe in legalized abortion only if they are to be performed by professional personnel who are trained in this medical skill.

Oddly enough, a great many of the womb perforations are chargeable to professional physicians. These are the physicians who lack basic training in the technique and use dangerous, sharp-pointed instruments with a callous disregard for correct procedures. Once abortion is legalized in a number of American states, I trust the medical schools will recognize the lack of training in this particular branch of expertise.

The complete legalization of abortion—and I believe it will come before too many more years—will mean the end of the unskilled, untrained practitioners.

Abortion, practiced openly by those who understand it and have developed the necessary skills, will with legalization be lifted from the dirty backstairs room to the antiseptic operating room where it belongs as a legitimate and often necessary surgical procedure.

CHAPTER TWENTY-FOUR

"The law, in its majestic equality," wrote Anatole France, "forbids the rich as well as the poor to sleep under bridges, to beg in the streets and to steal bread."

The French novelist's wit has a note of irony for those of us concerned with state laws forbidding abortion. Abortion, under the majestic (and too often archaic) statutes of the various states, is denied not only to the capricious but to the victim of rape, the pregnant woman suffering with thalidomide poisoning and those for whom childbirth can only mean hardship and suffering.

When one looks at the ancient laws of all kinds which still clutter the statute books he cannot but wonder if Charles Dickens' character was right when he said the "law is an ass." Customs and more change, but laws continue to exist no matter how outmoded. Slowest of all to change, it seems, are those laws rooted in church tradition which govern various sex practices. One can almost believe that those sturdy pioneers who framed most of these archaic laws were, in fact, obsessed with the subject of sex.

It is a crime in Maryland, for example, to sell contraceptives from a vending machine, unless the machine is located in a liquor store.

In Mississippi it is illegal to advertise, display, distribute or sell contraceptives. Yet, if a woman who had already had one illegitimate pregnancy, failed to go to a Planned Parenthood Center to obtain contraceptive material, she would be subject to heavy criminal penalties. In other words, Mississippi law can force a woman to commit an illegal act.

In South Dakota there is a law which forbids a woman, more than 50, to speak to a married man above the age of 20 on a street or sidewalk.

A law, still on the books in Pasadena, California, makes it illegal for a businessman to be alone in the office with a woman secretary.

Nebraska has a law which makes it an offense for a man to swear in the presence of a woman, but it is not illegal for a woman to swear in the presence of a male.

Hard to believe, but in Oxford, Ohio, it is unlawful for a woman to disrobe in the presence of a man's photograph.

In Challis, Idaho, it is an offense against an ordinance for a man to walk down the street accompanied by a woman other than his wife.

An Arizona statute makes it illegal for a wife to retain her own salary. She must turn it over to her husband.

It is a crime for anyone, including married couples, to kiss in the public parks of Chicago, Illinois.

Did you know there is a Kentucky law which forbids a man from marrying his wife's grandmother?

And there is a law in Shreveport, Louisiana, which makes it illegal for anyone to carry a concealed crochet needle—a law which, to an abortionist who knows what can happen to even the best ladies from the best sewing circles, is not as strange as it might seem.

The Oregon law under which I was convicted and sent to jail was written 103 years ago in 1864 and was modeled after an even earlier New York Law. It reads:

"If any person shall administer to any woman pregnant with child any medicine, drug or substance whatever, or shall use or employ any instrument or other means, with intent thereby to destroy such child, unless the same shall be necessary to preserve the life of such mother, such person shall, in case of the death of such child or mother thereby produced, be deemed guilty of manslaughter."

The phraseology of this law was broad because Oregon was still a raw, pioneer state. It was still the era of the medicine man and the midwife and there was no medical code, no regulation or licensing of the practice of medicine. Anyone could practice medicine. The abortion law was meant to include doctors and laymen alike.

Twenty-five years later, in 1889, the Oregon legislators adopted the state's first medical code. It created a board of medical examiners, provided for the licensing of physicians and surgeons and, among other things, provided for the revocation of the license of a doctor found guilty of unprofessional or dishonorable conduct. It did not define these terms, however. And it was silent on the subject of abortions.

In 1937, the legislature amended the medical practice act by defining unprofessional and dishonorable conduct on the part of a physician and surgeon as meaning:

"... the procuring or aiding and abetting in procuring an abortion, unless such is done for the relief of a woman whose health appears in peril, because of her pregnant condition, after due consultation with another licensed medical physicians and surgeon."

In 1939, the legislature further amended the medical practice act by defining an abortion in accordance with the Medical Code definition, i.e.:

"Abortion means the expulsion of the foetus at a period of uterogestation so early that it has not acquired the power of sustaining an independent life; provided it shall be conclusively presumed, for the purpose of this statute, that the foetus has not acquired such power earlier than 150 days after gestation and a disputable presumption of the lack of such power shall arise if the expulsion takes place earlier than 240 days after gestation."

A further amendment of the medical practice act came in 1951 when the Oregon legislature enacted law requiring a physician and surgeon, before performing an abortion, to consult a licensed physician and surgeon who "is not an associate or relative," and "who agrees that an abortion is necessary."

The Oregon Supreme Court several years ago reversed the conviction of a Portland physician and surgeon on a charge of "manslaughter by abortion," holding in a 4 to 3 split-decision that an abortion, to save the life of a pregnant woman under the criminal abortion act, and to preserve the health of a pregnant woman under the medical practices act, are lawful. All other abortions, said the court, are unlawful.

It is interesting to note that the dissenting minority opinion, written by Justice Brand and concurred in by Justices Lusk and Warner, took direct issue with the majority. These justices contended that the medical practices act neither amended nor partially repealed the 1864 criminal abortion act as to physicians and surgeons. They averred that the medical practices act was only a disciplinary measure and that the criminal abortion act was in full force and effect as to physicians and surgeons as well as to naturopaths, chiropractors, and all the other persons. They expressed heavy doubts as to the constitutionality of the criminal abortion act, as held by the majority of opinion.

It seems to me that this divided decision alone is sufficient reason for the Oregon Legislature to look to its statute housekeeping, throw out an 1864 abortion act from a puritanical era and bring Oregon—an enlightened state in most respects—abortion law reform with constructive, modern legislation.

As this book goes to press, Colorado, North Carolina and California have all taken long, forward strides in the field of abortion law reform. But even in these states the termination of pregnancy has been legalized only in narrowly defined situations such as rape and incest and where a full-term pregnancy would gravely threaten the mother's mental or physical health. I welcome these new laws as symptomatic of a changing public attitude toward my life's work, but I believe they still dodge the basic issue, i.e., the right of the individual women to determine privately what is best for her and then carry out that decision safely and with dignity.

Religious leaders have laid down the wholly unilateral fiat

that abortion is tantamount to homicide. Inflexible, discriminatory and, at times, irrational, they have spread a fanciful rationale based on both outmoded and flawed Biblical doctrine which has little to do with modern-day sociological problems.

Nearly 200 years ago, the August 1787 issue of London's "European Magazine" asked: "How long must man—weak and miserable man—wander through the wilds of prejudice and rebel against the authority of scared truth? Not surely, till he ceases to judge of virtues and of vice by their names."

I submit that abortion is not a four-letter word, nor is it a dirty name for an evil act. It is an operation performed, almost entirely illegally, on an estimated more than 1,000,000 American women each year.

It seems to me that it is more than time that this country's religious, medical and governmental leaders took cognizance of the obvious and made this necessary, minor surgical procedure freely available to those women who desire it.

CHAPTER
TWENTY-FIVE

It's time to get back to my story which I dropped five chapters back—not the way a woman drops a stich when knitting, for it was deliberate enough—to tell you just a little about the sociological and historical aspects of a much-maligned vocation.

You know, I could fill a book twice this size with the information about abortion I have gathered over the years. And some day, if I live long enough, I plan to write another book with the kind of background material which students of such matters might find useful in their researches. However, this book was not meant for the researcher but for lay readers, particularly the women, all kinds of women, to whom it is dedicated.

As I mentioned earlier, after my release from Rocky Butte jail in 1958 I was reduced to a much smaller practice, conducted on a necessarily clandestine basis. True, I was left pretty much alone by the authorities for eight years. But the number of women I was able to help was reduced to a relative trickle.

I took only those cases which were referred to me by physicians or by old and trusted friends and a few others where I was so convinced of the patient's desperation that I threw my usual caution to the winds. My big fat sympathetic nerve was to get me in trouble again.

I'm grateful for the eight years I was let alone. It was good, after the storm and stress of the '50's to have a little peace and quiet. I bought a small condominium in Hawaii and went there for short vacations, but not as often as I would have liked. I spent a great deal of time with my grandchildren and fussed over my dogs. Every now and then I would entertain friends at home—you'd be surprised at some of my friends, for I like all kinds of people, including some not acceptable in "polite society"—and, aging gal that I was, I still managed a night "on the town" from time to time.

In December of 1964 a large mole on my left leg began to bleed. I had had the mole for 40 years and it had never given me a great deal of grief. Before my doctor finished his biopsy, I suspected what his diagnosis would be—malignant melanoma.

I was in hospital for a month, including the Christmas and New Year's holidays, while the mole was excised. It healed up nicely, but I knew chances were that the cancer would show up elsewhere before too long.

In February I went to Honolulu for a short vacation and convalescence and after I returned to Portland, I was lying in bed one night, pulled at my nightdress and felt a swelling in my groin. "There it is," I said to myself. The next day I was back at my doctor's office.

"I don't suppose you'll let me operate?" my doctor asked.

"At my age?" I exclaimed. "You know, Doctor, if I had it to do over I wouldn't' have let you cut out the mole."

He realized I was firm with no further operations, so he arranged for me to go to the Swedish Hospital in Seattle—a marvelous institution where they use the last techniques for combating cancerous tumors with considerable success, including oxygen under very high pressures.

My first trip to Seattle was in the spring of 1965 and since then I've been up there for eight further treatments. They seem to have been of great value, but one can never been sure. These melanomas spread to the glands, the lungs and the brain and I have been getting regular X-Rays and keeping my fingers crossed.

In July of 1965, I purchased a large motel in downtown Portland. This motel, to my mind, was purely and investment for the future of my grandchildren. There was considerable fuss over the licensing of the motel because of my previous con-

THEY WEEP ON MY DOORSTEP

THEY WEEP ON MY DOORSTEP

victions. Apparently, some members of the Portland police department had convinced the Portland City Council that I was going to use the motel as some kind of "front" for my abortion practice.

The simple truth is that I made it very plain from the outset that the motel was to have no connection of any kind with my practice. A trusted friend and onetime associate took over management of the motel, once I had council approval for the purchase, and ever since has done a splendid job of keeping it free from taint of any kind. It is not easy in the hotel or motel business to keep undesirables from occasionally securing lodging, but my people have been most circumspect. At times, they may have been a little too rigid in their requirements. One unaccompanied woman guest we discreetly asked to give up a room because we were so eager to make sure the police could find no fault of any kind with the operation, turned out to be a respectable woman in the city for a series of examinations at the University of Oregon Medical School—the very thing she had told our desk clerk. My manager had a telephone call from her physician who was most unhappy about our asking her to leave. My motel staff was able to apologize and make amends for the over zealousness in rigid innkeeping.

It is because I was so insistent that the motel not have any connection with my other activity that I was most perturbed by something that happened late in 1965. But I am getting just a bit ahead of my narrative.

On January 14, 1966, a group of Multnomah County detectives came to my home near Washington Park. They had a search warrant and two warrants for my arrest on manslaughter abortion charges. I should have realized—I suppose I did realize —that I could not continue my practice indefinitely immune from arrest. In 1964 the voters of my county elected a new district attorney who was both extremely young and politically most ambitious. I do not censure him for doing his job which is, of course, to enforce whatever laws he is supposed to enforce. And I doubt that, looking back, I would have curbed my practice even had I realized that it might end in further trouble with the law. (My attorney has often remarked that I am a rational woman in all other matters of life, but he questions my sanity on the subject of my chosen vocation. He even suggested, more than half-seriously, that he could plead me "insane" on this one subject because he says even though I know of the existence of the law, have been arrested, convicted and incarcerated because of the law, I continue to defy it.)

I was, as I said earlier, most upset when I learned certain facts about the case which brought my arrest. The couple, an assistant instructor from Oregon State University, and his pregnant girlfriend, a home economics teacher from a junior college in California, had spent the night at my motel, registered as husband and wife. Their staying there, as far as I can determine, was pure coincidence. But I was most unhappy about the implication that there was somehow a connection between their being registered there and her subsequent visit to my home.

Because this particular case, along with more recent cases against me, is currently on appeal to the higher courts, I have been advised by counsel to not comment on certain aspects of it. I would just like to state simple and briefly that I did not perform an abortion on the Los Angeles teacher. I did make an examination. It was obvious to anyone of my experience that someone else had tampered with the girl's uterus before I made my examination. I have no way of knowing who it was.

The jury found me guilty of manslaughter by abortion and the court, apparently mindful of my earlier convictions, sentenced me to 18 months in the Oregon State prison. My appeal is still pending.

In none of my trials have I been able to take the witness stand in my own defense. The reasons for this must be obvious. None of my lawyers have ever been so rash as to ask me to take the stand. They have, indeed, insisted that I do not, as in my right under the law. When any person is accused of any crime the burden of proving the crime is on the state. In my case there would be particular jeopardy in taking the stand. For one thing,

I am a forthright woman and would most likely give candid answers to any questions put to me by the prosecutor. A clever prosecutor could use this trait of mine to the state's advantage, asking questions which might incriminate me in the minds of the jurors. Added to this is the equally obvious fact that, by my own admission, I have been engaged for nearly 50 years in a profession considered illegal and anything I said about it would most likely only serve to damn me at the bar of justice.

In October of 1966 I was on a trial again. This was a particularly messy case. The patient, an Albany, Oregon woman, was described in court as a virtual nymphomaniac. She was impregnated by a man on parole from a federal person sentence. This woman lied on the witness stand, stating that she had no previous abortions, finally admitting after cross-examination that she had twice undergone induced abortion previously.

My attorneys made an eloquent plea in this case for the jurors to find me guilty of the lesser office of "attempted abortion," but the jury, nevertheless, convicted me of the more serious count. This time the judge handed me a two-year prison sentence and a fine of $5,000.

In sentencing me, Circuit Judge Robert E. Jones stipulated that if I were, indeed, suffering a terminal cancer as my attorneys had told the court, he would recommend my release from prison before I served the full term. "If the cancer is terminal," said Judge Jones, "I will ask that the warden release her early so that she can spend her last days at home."

In his appeal of this case, yet to be heard by the Oregon Supreme Court, my attorney has presented some interesting questions. One is whether a woman who knowingly solicits another and participates, aids and abets the commission of an unlawful abortion, and submits her body for its perpetration, is a principal and an accomplice under the provisions of an Oregon statute which states: "All persons concerned in the commission of a felony or aid and abet in its commission, are principals?" He has cited numerous points and authorities in law to support this contention. Among them the ruling of Lord Adkins in Australia v. Barclay (Appeal Cases 1-29 1941):

"When the ghosts of the past stand in the path of justice clanking their medieval chains, the proper course for the judge is to pass through them undeterred."

My appellate lawyer, Mr. Leo Levenson, has argued: "A woman may be the victim of a man who seduces her under the promise of marriage or some fictionists promise; she may be duped or cheated by a house-to-house peddler and a victim in believing his fabulous promises. But how can it be argued, in good faith, that where she initiates, solicits and knowingly and willingly conspires to aid and abet another to commit an offense, that she is a virtuous victim, but the other person a culprit. In what manner is she a victim, and of whom?"

"Why is it just, in this enlightened era, to indulge in specious reasoning by holding that a matured (sic) woman, as is — —, who had previously undertaken two other abortions, is a victim? She is the person who instigated and promoted the commission of the offense. She is the person who has the criminal intent; she is the one who solicits, aids, abets, counsels and is *concerned* in the commission of the offense. Without her, there would indeed, be no crime committed!"

Mr. Levenson is a learned man as well as an able lawyer and he added to his appeal brief several "authorities" not usually cited in legal matters. Among them, the anthropologist Ashley Montagu:

"Having successfully freed herself for her thralldom to man, woman has now to emancipate herself from the myth of inferiority, and to realize her potentialities to the fullest."

Again, he quotes from Betty Friedan's "The Feminine Mystique": "But there would be no sense in my writing this book at all if I did not believe that woman can affect society, as well as be affected by it; that, in the end, a woman as a man, has the power to choose, and to make her own heaven or hell."

In this same case, my attorney has raised the question in his appeal of the lower court's objection to asking questions of prospective jurors concerning their religious affiliations.

The Oregon State Constitution provides that no person shall be rendered incompetent as a witness or juror in consequence of his opinions on matters of religion, nor be questioned in any court of justice touching his religious belief.

But my lawyer argues that this constitutional provision is not applicable to the voir dire examination of prospective jurymen. He suggests that the religious faith or lack of inquiry, enabling a more intelligent use of the defendant's right of peremptory challenge.

"We submit," argues Mr. Levenson, "that there are emotional factors which direct and, to a large extent, control human responses.... Each person is a separate entity because he alone is the sum total of his experiences and beliefs... The right of an accused to a trial by an impartial jury is of little advantage if the jury has come from a religious group biased and prejudiced by influences which he is unable to countervail."

For the first time in the history of Oregon jurisprudence, my lawyer is seeking a high court ruling on a fundamental question of the jury system. Mincing no words, his brief urges the Oregon Supreme Court to take "judicial knowledge of a fact that Catholic theology identifies abortion with murder... tied up(in the minds of prospective jurors) deep in their emotional lives with an interlocking claim of other emotionally loaded subjects: sex, womanhood, marriage, motherhood, good and evil, right and wrong," making an intelligent use of the right of peremptory challenge impossible if no inquiry as to religious affiliated is permitted.

Following the 1966 arrests, I realized it was quite impossible for me to continue performing operations at my home. I was obviously under constant surveillance Anda could not ask my patients to risk the embarrassment of any further "raids." Hence, I bought a home outside of jurisdiction of Multnomah County.

Located on McLoughlin Boulevard in Clackamas County, the new premised offered a pleasant and more clinical atmosphere to do my work. I would sometimes meet patients at the new address, or, in some cases, take them to the Clackamas County. I was hopeful, perennial optimist that I am, that I could carry on there without legal interference.

But such as not to be. In February of 1967 the Clackamas County grand jury indicted me on still another charge of manslaughter by abortion. This was followed by a second, and then, a third charge.

As I write these final chapters I still await trial on the Clackamas County charges. I have heard that the State of Oregon has moving picture films made with a concealed movie camera outside my Clackamas County quarters. These films purportedly show the license numbers of automobiles which visited my place. Using these license numbers, diligent investigators have tracked down a number of women patients, some of whom have given testimony to the grand jury.

A few weeks ago, I sold my Clackamas County property. I have also moved from my Portland home of the past 20 years and it is up for sale. I have bought a new home and recently, I held a wedding reception there for my granddaughter and namesake.

My future is not particularly auspicious at the moment. No matter how you slice it, it's strictly hard cheese.

CHAPTER
TWENTY-SIX

This old gal is near the end of life's highway and nobody knows it better than she.

It's not just that my 75th birthday is looming ahead. I've always been as strong as a horse and I may have had another 10 years, give or take a few.

But the old girl is carrying some renegade cells around in a body that, until a few years ago, had never let her down.

It's ironic, isn't it? The cancer will most likely get me before the warden at the Oregon state penitentiary.

At the moment there are already an 18-months prison sentence and a two-year prison sentence chalked up against me. If my appeals against these convictions fail, I could be going to the penitentiary for two years or more.

And I still face the trials scheduled in Clackamas County. On the basis of my track record, which hasn't been exactly brilliant, I can expect still further prison sentences if the juries find me guilty in those cases.

But I don't wish to dwell on what may never be. I've never been much of a worrier and it's no time now to start crossing bridges before I reach them.

However, as I write this final chapter to a book, I have neglected far too long, I can't resist a backward look. Yes, I am well aware that my life, like this book, is swiftly moving to a final page.

And so, I ask myself, what kind of a life has it been, Dr. Ruth? Have you accomplished anything, old girl, in those 75 years?

Will you leave any kind of legacy behind you? Adding up the accounts, where do you stand?

These aren't easy questions for me. I've never been much of one for philosophy.

Regrets? Yes, I have my share. My personal life has not been all that it could have been. My marriages were, when viewed in retrospect, something less than perfect.

Surely, I erred badly in being overly indulgent with my daughter. Her life has been fraught with tragedy and unhappiness. And a great deal of her unhappiness has been, in turn, visited upon me. I do wish there were some way at least a portion of all that misery could be undone.

Things have gone better with my grandchildren. As a mother I learned a few lessons which I have, I trust, made me a better grandmother. And I hope their lives will be less story, less troubled. We always wish tranquility for those we love, knowing that few persons ever find real peace.

When I evaluate my own life, I think of it as pretty much like a credit and a debit ledger. And heading the credit side of the ledger are the friends I've managed to make and hold over the years. When you've been arrested vilified by the newspapers and thrown in jail, you find out who your real friends are. And I've been able to muster a whole battalion right through all the troubles.

Strong though my belief in the rightness of abortion has been, I have not been blind about the effect my views may have had on those more concerned with the niceties of such outmoded law than I. For instance, I have pushed myself on no one. I have never made application to join a private club. I didn't wish to embarrass any of my friends, and I didn't wish to impose on those whom I knew would have gone to bat for me. I'm not much of a joiner, anyway.

My life has been illuminated with a lot of bright spots. When I think how low I was at the time of my first arrest, I also remember the joy that was mine when I first acquired the Stewart Clinic. When I recall the harshness of the judges and juries, I also recollect the women of leading families who have come to me for my services—and I remember the leading physicians, surgeons and gynecologists who sent them to me.

To my way of thinking, society has dealt a little harshly with me at times. After all, it's hard for me to see the justice in being sent to prison doing society a favor.

Before I finish my story, I'd like to say a word about those few people who have called me "Ruthless Ruth." You know, ironically enough, that's a name I hung on myself. With my sense of humor, it seemed as though it was a joke on me. But a few people have been meaning enough to use the epithet in a derogatory way.

This spring, of course, from the contention that I have charged large fees for my services. Prosecutors have repeatedly stressed my fees in addressing juries. There are several things I wish to say about that.

First of all, I have never, in 50 years of practice, ever solicited a case. The women who wished operations came to me. I did my work well and I charged what I believe was a fair price for the operation. And I've also done a lot of operations without a fee.

The laborer is worthy of his hire and so it is with each professional service that is rendered in the marketplace. Not long ago, I paid a surgeon $2,500 to excise a malignant mole from my leg. I did not carp or criticize his fee. That is his profession and he is entitled to charge for his skill and knowledge.

Furthermore, I think the public should know that my chosen vocation has proved both an expensive and hazardous one. For more than 25 years now, I spent countless hours in the courtroom. I have spent many days conferring with lawyers. And I have paid out more than $100,000 in attorney's fees, and the legal costs of my appeals.

As I near the end of my career, I am, if anything, more convinced than ever of the moral and ethical right of abortions. A woman's body is her own personal and private responsibility.

I have been asked if I believe in abortion as a means of birth control. I certainly do, where such control is indicated, either for economic reasons or reasons of health.

In a way, I've been running my own personal planned parenthood program—and without the expense of administrative personnel. Do you think the physicians of America are opposed to such a form of birth control? I wish we could tell you how many doctors have sent their wives to me.

The doctors don't really know all the possible results of continuous use of "the pill." For how many years can a woman take the pill and not suffer any ill effects? It is still too new for this to be measured. It is my considered opinion that safe, swift abortion is less hazardous to a woman than the use of birth control pills. There will show whether I am correct in such an assumption.

The truth is that medical science has not yet devised a really safe, sure, convenient means of birth control. I have a little joke I used to tell patients about a "glass of buttermilk" being the only really effective birth control measure. "Don't take it either before or after," I'd tell them. "Take it instead."

I am greatly encouraged as I conclude this book by the developments this year in the state legislatures of California, North Carolina and Colorado, all of which have at long last liberalized their abortion statutes. I have no doubt that other states will follow in the years to co me. Before too long, I believe, most American states, along with the world's other enlightened governments, will permit qualified persons to perform this simple operation for all women who wish it, whatever the reason.

And it is worth noting that in many countries the pendulum of public opinion is swinging away from superstition and medieval dogma and towards enlightenment and legal reform. Not long ago in "The Living Church," a magazine published by the Episcopalian Church, I noted that in Great Britain a sizable group of person is urging abortion law reform, some going as far as to suggest "that abortion be permissible at the will of the mother." This group, along with millions of Americans, is aware that a woman's capacity, as a wife and mother, can and often is severely overtaxed by the birth of another child.

The case for the unmarried mother is equally strong. Pregnancy waits upon biology, not upon law. There is wisdom in the old law that a marriage may be delayed, but not the baby.

Meanwhile, my telephone continues to ring. I get calls from women in distress late into the night. They come not only from Oregon women, but from women in Salt Lake City, Spokane and Wichita, Kansas. After I am gone, I do not know who will get these telephones calls, but they will go to someone.

Millions of American women have had abortions. Millions more will seek such operations in the future. My sympathies will remain with them as long as I live because I have known their plight. And I have known also what it is to be helped in such a situation and to face life anew.

So, while the laws against abortion remain, your duty is clear. If you believe as I do, that abortion is a matter of personal decision, then you must rise up and demand a change in the laws.

Until major changes in the laws are brought about, my duty is also clear. As long as I am able I must take care of those who come to weep on my doorstep.

EPILOGUE

It has been nearly 18 months since I wrote what I thought was the last line of this book. In some ways, I wish that the book could have ended with that unhappy yet proud declaration that I would continue to care for those who came to weep on my doorstep. But such was not to be.

On February 5, 1968, I entered the Oregon women's penitentiary to begin serving a two-year sentence on charges of manslaughter by abortion. My attorney had exhausted his appeals to the Oregon Supreme Court and there was nothing left for me but to make the best of it. I had thought that my physical condition might win me another stay of sentence, but the law is remorseless. At 74, I was the oldest woman ever incarcerated by the State of Oregon.

I am not going to tell you that I enjoyed my first (and last!) sojourn in the Beaver State's modern correctional institution for women. On the other hand, I'm not going to tell you that it was any nightmare, either. In all truth, it is the finest place that any such institution can be. It has been dubbed Oregon's "country club" and the nickname is not a cruel joke, but a tribute to a really excellent penal facility.

Country club or not, prison still prison. When I arrived, I had to surrender even the few things I had brought with me. They took my wig my false eyelashes and had me take a shower. A man took my fingerprints. My fingers went crack, crack, crack, as he rolled them over the inky form. "My you have lots of arthritis," he said.

They gave me an almost unbelievable cotton nightie. I hadn't seen one like it since I was a girl in Hood River. One of the matrons gave me a little sample lipstick to do me until I could buy one at the commissary later in the week.

They brought me a uniform with a Peter Pan collar and a big pair of ugly Buster Brown shoes. I couldn't bear the shoes and after a few days one of the matrons brought me a pair of tennis shoes. I washed them inside and out with shampoo soap and cleaned the shoelaces with Bon Ami and they weren't at all bad.

That first day there was a wonderful food to eat and I soon learned that the 51 women with whom I shared the prison ate well every day. We had spaghetti and meatballs the very first day and salad and chocolate pie and cornbread and hot biscuits. There were pancakes every morning. No wonder nearly all the inmates had big bottoms.

The second day I had my X-rays and a lot of vaccinations and inoculations. They gave me shots for polio, diphtheria, flu and tetanus and I got a terrible reaction. I was feverish for six days. I just lay in bed and read a little. Three mornings I was too sick to take the compulsory shower. Before the fever broke, I lost 13 pounds.

But after those six dreadful days, it wasn't at all bad. My 51 fellow inmates were all kind to me, and the matrons were nice to everybody. The girls would grab my tray at mealtimes and help me with it because of my cane. We were all sisters under the skin.

Each girl has a private room, about nine feet by 10 feet. They are designed so that there are no bars showing anywhere, just cottage windows. There is a birch door with a little glass spy-hole so the matrons can look in.

After a while I wrote in my diary, "If I could just sleep nights, everything would be jake. Time doesn't worry me. The days fly by. I paid a couple of thousands of dollars one time to send my daughter to a luxury place in California to lose weight—this beats it all over."

Another day I wrote: "The ducks and geese fly over and I wonder why the guard in the tower doesn't take a shot at them. He sits up there all day and I wonder if he has a grudge against the world or just against himself."

While I spent my days cleaning my room—I used a rag on the end of my cane to clean under my bed—and reading Frank Yerby and Phillip Wylie novels—life went on in the outside world. My Marine grandson was hit by a shrapnel in Vietnam, two of his best buddies blown up right beside him. They brought him to the states and my granddaughter Ruthie, and her husband went down to California to see him. Ruthie wrote me every other day and one day there was other bad news—my little Yorkie, Tiger, had been run over and killed. That really hit me, and I had a couple of very bad days and nights.

And then there were the days when Martin Luther King was killed and when Bobby Kennedy was killed. They let us watch the funerals on television and it was sad. And it was sad when some of the girls were discharged and they left with nobody to pick them up and hardly anything in the way of clothes. They seemed terribly lonely to me.

Several of the inmates were particularly kind to me. There was a huge black woman I'll call "Trina" who fixed me nice trays and smuggled me oranges from the kitchen. She was in for bad check charges. She was one of the two inmates who always called me, "Doctor." When I finally discharged, she couldn't bear to watch me leave.

And there was a girl I'll call "Betty" who did my ironing for me. It hurt me to do my own dresses. There was a pathetic girl who looked like a schoolteacher. She had put her baby in a bathtub and slit its throat. Her other children saw her, so she killed them, too. She had been in and out of the State hospital as insane and serving a life sentence. There was a very quiet girl working in the kitchen who was the girlfriend of a girl who had killed her children.

Of all the things that happened while I was at Salem, I think one of the most amusing was when the girls found out about my using shoe polish from the commissary on my hair. I was allergic to hair dyes and the polish worked beautifully. When the girls found out about it they laughed uproariously and the next morning I found a note shoved under my door:

"Ruth, my dear... What brings you here?.. A law we must abolish.. But I do quite well... So, what the hell... With my cane and can of polish."

And so the months went by with clean sheets once a week, clean towels twice a week, lots of Scrabble games and a number of girls taking the Upward Bound classes in the north wing. The matrons were capable and strict for discipline, but fair. There were bouquets of flowers from the greenhouse at the men's prison. It wasn't too bad/

On Saturday, March 9, there was a major riot at the men's prison. My room in the west wing faced the wall and at 3 o'clock in the morning I could look out the window and see the flames shooting up. I counted 15 yellow raincoats which I took to be state policemen.

There were only two matrons on duty on Saturdays and the girls were nervous and muttering. Quite a few of them had been arrested with their "old men" and those "old men" were in the regular prison and they were concerned about them. I was playing Scrabble when we first heard about it and one of them said to me, "Maybe we should riot a little." I said, "You will not." But the girls were upset and nervous, so the matrons decided to let them dance. Ordinarily, dancing is forbidden because they don't want girls to have body contact. But the girls danced the night and Trina, the big black woman, went to the kitchen and made a big batch of popcorn. We got through the riot without any real trouble in the women's prison.

During the five and one-half months I was in the penitentiary a lot of good people on the outside were petitioning the parole board to consider my release. They raised the question of my age and the cancer of my legs. The parole board apparently shared the view of these persons that my imprisonment wasn't of any great value to the people of Oregon. On July 1, 1968, I went before those five solemn men.

They asked me some preliminary questions and then one of the men on board asked me what was one of the most difficult questions ever put to me: "Would you do me a favor and promise me you will never do another abortion?" is what he asked.

"Never?" I said. "Never is a long, long time. I'm never going to prison again for somebody else's delinquency."

"You were delinquent," he said.

"I was delinquent for 50 years," I said. But I could tell by the way he looked at me that I was either going to give him the right answer or I was going to be in prison a lot longer. It was no time for argument no time for any discussion of the rights and wrongs of abortion. It was my moment of truth and if I didn't handle it rightly I could well die in that jail.

He put that question again. "Would you promise me, Ruth? You're so well known that if you start operating again it would let us down."

I looked him right in the eye and I said, "I give you my sacred word of honor as a lady I'll never do another abortion."

"That's all we want," he said.

My heart jumped and I asked the board if I could get out for the fourth of July. But it wasn't that easy. There was a matter of paying a $5,000 fine adjudged in one of the cases and other technicalities. I was finally released on July 15.

So, I came home to my grandchildren and my dogs. I spend all my days like a lot of other grandmothers, except that I manage to do a lot of fishing. Not long ago we put nearly 500 pounds of tuna into our boat. There are still new thrills in life for me, even though I've reached my 75th birthday.

After 50 years living "outside" an unjust law, I now live within that law, as I promised the parole board I would. But while I keep my promise, I cannot alter my thinking about a law that I think belongs in the dustbin of history. Some day, with your help, such laws will be no more than past reminders of man's bottomless stupidity and monumental inertia in the face of social progress.

At 75, I cannot hope to see universal abortion law reform. But already, I see a glimmer of light and a bright hope for a better world for the woman of an enlightened tomorrow.

Made in United States
Orlando, FL
11 May 2022

17772906R00100